PRAISE FOR *HOW TO TALK TO TEACHERS*

Students benefit from knowing that their parents and teachers are working together to support their success both inside and outside the classroom. *How to Talk to Teachers* offers parents a positive and proactive guide on how to engage with their child's teacher and create a roadmap for effective collaboration between home and school. This partnership is essential so that every child receives the education necessary to ensure that they are future-ready.

– CAMILLE RUTHERFORD
Associate Professor, Faculty of Education,
Brock University (Ontario, Canada)

In a rapidly changing world where technological advancements are continuously disrupting the status quo, a positive parent-teacher partnership is pivotal, to help students become global citizens who thrive and reach their fullest potential. *How To Talk to Teachers* provides a comprehensive roadmap for nurturing a generation that is ready to face both the challenges and opportunities that come their way. An essential read for educators and parents alike.

–MARTHA JEZ
Parent and CEO of Fair Chance Learning

How to Talk to Teachers is a testament to the power of community in education, illustrating that when teachers and parents unite, they create a strong foundation for the future success of our children. Lia De Cicco Remu underscores the critical importance of a healthy partnership between parents and teachers in fostering a supportive and collaborative environment for student success. A must-read that is insightful, eloquent, and empathetic, this book is easy to read and full of tips for parents that will help guide conversations with teachers.

— JESSICA RIZK

Parent and Senior Research Associate, Education & Skills,
The Conference Board of Canada

HOW TO TALK TO TEACHERS

LIA DE CICCO REMU

ONYX PUBLISHING

First published in 2024 by Onyx Publishing, an imprint of Notebook
Group Limited, Arden House, Deepdale Business Park, Bakewell,
Derbyshire, DE45 1GT.

www.onyxpublishing.com
ISBN: 9781913206703

A CIP catalogue record for this book is available
from the British Library.

Typeset by Onyx Publishing of Notebook Group Limited.

To my first teacher, my mother.
To my greatest teacher, my daughter.
To my biggest love, my husband.

CONTENTS

INTRODUCTION

Today, our world is facing problem after problem, from climate change and super-viruses to unstable economies. Our kids will be tasked with navigating all of it.

It's our job, as educators, parents, and leaders, to create an environment in our school systems, right now, that will enable our children to evolve and be better to each other and our world. These kids are "woke", and it is us, the wisdom workers, who are here to "activate" them, safely and compassionately, and set them loose. It's time to give tomorrow's citizens a clear map and allow them to figure out where it takes them. They will have to navigate as far as they can, to roads or planets unknown, so we will need to help them as much as we can while we are still here.

In these pages and through my stories, we'll delve into what school was, what it is, and what it can be, to help parents like you understand why classrooms are what they are and what they could become. This book was written to give parents like you the tools and language they'll need to navigate our complicated education system; to support reflection and respectful, productive discussions with teachers.

Within these pages, you will find personal anecdotes, insights, and experiences working with educators and system leaders who are passionate about helping children succeed. This book is a reimagining of education from that vantage point, and it is an invitation to you, the reader, to help find solutions that will move us forward.

There is much work to be done.

I acknowledge that my experience doesn't reflect that of all parents, and I don't have the lens of the low income, disengaged, and/or racialized communities within our system. Still, my intention is and has always been to strive for equity, inclusion of all, and diverse perspectives in all the work that I do.

It's hard work to support your child's learning, in and out of school, in a way where they can fully grow into their best possible self. During my fifteen-plus-year career in education so far, many parents have approached me for help in this respect. I hope I've helped them, and I hope this book helps you, too.

Lia De Cicco Remu
Toronto, Canada

1

SCHOOL SUCKS

———

I WAS TOLD IN TEACHERS' COLLEGE I would never be an educator.

In all honesty, the program made little sense to me. I couldn't quite connect what was presented in the lectures to the teaching I knew I'd be doing in the field. At first, this contradiction was puzzling. It worried me. I wanted to help children learn and grow, but what I was learning didn't line up with the heart of my goal, which was (and still is) to help kids become their best selves; to become connected, contributing citizens that shine in the world. My lectures were more about the subject areas I was going to be teaching than they were about children.

Maybe I wasn't a teacher after all.

But no. I am hardheaded by nature and couldn't give up, so I kept going.

For my very first practicum, I asked to serve in a placement in one of most underserved and diverse schools in Toronto (Ontario, Canada). My request was granted, and off I went, determined and ready to learn how to be a teacher.

On the first day, I sat watching Mr. H, my mentor and a seasoned educator, "teach" a class of thirty-plus students. Day after day, these kids came to class and shared their stories with us. Some of these involved their townhouse complex being raided the night before, or the fact that they'd seen a real body bag leave by ambulance. They came to school bleary eyed and hungry. It was our job to make sure they fully understood Bernoulli's principle.

I know Mr. H cared deeply for his students, and in his mind, he was doing the best he could in his classroom. Yet he taught the way he had been taught to: in an atmosphere of fear and shame. As was not uncommon for the teachers of that time, he yelled frequently and repeatedly told the kids the reason they were failing was because they "didn't care about their education or their futures". The truth was, those twelve-year-olds were in survival mode. They had checked out because they had enough to deal with at home, never mind in school.

I sat there, heartbroken, on edge, and anxious during most of my placement. The classroom environment we create at school is critical for student engagement and success. If a child doesn't feel connected to their teacher or the material being presented, they'll feel no motivation to learn said material. All students need is to be heard and seen in safe spaces characterized by learning, inquiry, problem solving, and creativity. I knew this innately. Still, I soldiered on and prepared to teach my first math class *à la* Mr. H.

Textbook in hand and with my back to the students, I scratched a series of problems on a dusty chalkboard. I could hear scurrying, chairs scraping, whispers, and some snickering going on behind me. When I turned around, I "caught" two boys facing each other. They were "walking" their fingers on outstretched palms, which they would sometimes "blast off" into the air. I knew I was supposed to chastise them (in keeping with the teaching practice modeled to me), but in that moment, I cast aside any chance of getting an A from my mentor (along with any chance of me crossing the stage to graduate teachers' college) and simply stopped the lesson. "Hey, D," I said to the ringleader. "What are you guys doing?"

"Nothing, Miss."

I pressed on. "That looks pretty cool. What are you doing?"

There was absolutely no trust between me and the students at this point. That's exactly what I was trying to establish. I had to let them know I was on their side and genuinely interested in what they were playing (which I was).

I waited and waited. And then: "They're hops, Miss."

What on earth was a hop? Boy oh boy, I certainly wasn't teaching math anymore. I was sure "hops" wasn't one of the curricular outcomes I was supposed to be delivering. Still, my gameplan was to understand these kids first; to align their interests with the math I was teaching so they could find themselves in it. The last thing these hungry, agitated children needed was to snap at attention to me. No. They needed to connect to me, and I needed to connect their personal experiences to their learning, to make it relevant. If I could make math personal, they would be less bored and disinterested.

It worked.

Stepping away from the blackboard, I kickstarted a dialogue in a curious, kind, and nonjudgemental way. Within minutes, the whole class came alive. Good thing I could still do a layup, because these kids wanted to talk basketball. They were counting how many broad steps they needed to take to get a bucket, how many for a short drive in the key, and how many from outside the line.

I took that bit of info and the language they were using and integrated it into my math lesson. Now we were on track. I included everyone, and even those who weren't athletes became engaged, simply because I chose to use their names in the material I referenced.

This spirit—this collaborative energy—spilled beyond math, to science, literacy, and gym. For any child having difficulty with the material or facing social challenges, this small strategy made a difference.

We were onto something.

The Past: "It Was Good Enough for Me"

I get a kick out of giving kids old rotary phones, floppy disks, and CDs, and watching them try to understand the purpose of each item. We've seen this done on the Internet, and it's really funny. Our kids don't listen to music how we did when we were their age, nor do we talk or share information the same way. Above all, we don't connect the same way. Everything has changed so drastically that we (the parents) are the ones playing catchup with our children.

The same is true for learning delivery in schools right now. We know that today's parent had a different schooling experience and grew up in a vastly different landscape compared to how their kids are growing up now. I've come across many well-meaning parents who, when questioned on the effectiveness of our current, out-of-date teaching pedagogy, assert, "It was good enough for me," and that they don't feel as though they were failed by the system, and so their children should do just as well or better with the same setup. However, there's a lot of backstory that provides perspective on why we are in the pickle we are in—why so many of our kids are struggling with and disengaged from school—and that provides insight into how we can move forward.

All students deserve better than "good enough", and all unique learners are special. Up to high school graduation (not including kindergarten), students spend approximately six and a half hours a day, one hundred days a year, for twelve years, in school. That's a whopping fourteen thousand and forty hours of their lives in a walled place we call school. That's a lot of time to spend wishing you were playing basketball instead!

School isn't supposed to be a punishment, but a place for exploration and growth. I, for one, was the kid who loved it. I could play the game and take a test successfully. But alas, that's not the case for a lot of children. So many events, policy changes, and educational philosophies, along with differences in race, class, gender, and rural versus urban education, have shaped school as it exists today. That's another book for the researchers and policymakers, and they know all this stuff anyway. What we, as parents, need to understand is how and what kids have been taught up until now, and we need to question whether current teaching and learning practice reflects the cultural beliefs and economic needs of the times. We need to break down the historical purpose of education so that us parents can connect the dots, understand how to navigate our educational system today, and, ultimately, provide our kids with the best possible learning experiences.

School, today, is supposed to help children become connected, contributing citizens of humanity, but it hasn't always been that way. Way back in the 1700s, young white men were being schooled to:

1. Build their moral and ethical development.
2. Establish and maintain social control and order.
3. Understand basic literacy and numeracy.
4. Become religious leaders.
5. Preserve cultural heritage.

Let's jump to the mid to late nineteenth century and see what went down then, because the developments during this time laid the foundation for the modern educational system kids (*your* kids) experience today.

Nineteenth Century Schooling

It was a transformative period, with the budding practice of public schooling, compulsory education for children, standardized schools for teacher training, and increased access to education for various segments of society. Education was no longer limited to the elite or the privileged few. Religious and moral education still had its place in the curriculum, and basic subjects such as reading, writing, arithmetic, and history also began to be emphasized. Instruction was mostly rote based, centring on memorization and recitation.

I bet that students from that period were better spellers than our kids are today, and that they knew the answer to twelve multiplied by eight off the tops of their heads. But were these the "good old days" of education? Park this idea. We'll investigate whether these skills are truly as important as we think later in this book.

The nineteenth century also brought us a more child-centered approach, emphasizing hands-on learning and the addition of practical experiences.

There was a significant wave of immigration to North America during this time, and schools had to accommodate students like me, from diverse backgrounds and languages. This led to challenges in education and, in turn, the development of bilingual and multicultural education programs in some areas (and the acceptance of the stinky mortadella sandwiches I brought for lunch, or the pungent curries and tofu of other immigrant kids!). With these new approaches came the expansion of educational opportunities for groups that had previously been marginalized. Women's colleges were established, and greater access to education was provided for black students (although segregation and discrimination continued to persist).

Twentieth Century Schooling

When I went to university in the 1980s, I was astounded by the fact that a mere ten years prior, women still hadn't been allowed inside certain buildings. Meanwhile, I, the daughter of Italian immigrants, had the opportunity to attend university and be educated beyond the first- to fourth-grade schoolhouse learning my parents had left behind in their home country.

The idea of providing education to all children became increasingly important during the twentieth century. Many countries implemented policies to achieve universal primary education, the goal being to ensure that every child had access to schooling. We began to recognize the rights of individuals with disabilities and to include students with special needs in mainstream education, leading to the development of special education programs and the concept of inclusive education (emphasis on "concept", as we don't have this right just yet).

When industrialization following World War II became a thing, vocational education became increasingly important, and schools began to offer specialized training to prepare students for specific trades or professions, reflecting the changing needs of the workforce.

Twenty-First Century Schooling

Now, let's take a breath for a second. Think about whether school *today* reflects the changing needs of the workforce.

Kids still take a lot of tests. Some still sit in rows. Many complete worksheets and memorize facts (like in the nineteenth and twentieth century). Tests initially emerged as a method to assess student performance and evaluate educational outcomes, and testing has become more and more prevalent. It is still used to measure the effectiveness of schools and teachers. In the United States, for example, the dreaded SAT (Scholastic Assessment Test) and other standardized tests have been widely used for the college admissions process for years.

Current assessment practice makes me nuts.

Some important seeds were planted in the twentieth century school system, even though schools were predominantly focused on producing good factory workers, because that's what the economy needed then. Kids were taught the skills underpinning manual labour, like punctuality, competency with repetitive tasks, following instructions, producing maximum output, and not overthinking too much. These are good things. However, the twentieth century is not the world your little ones live in now. We need to move with the times.

We are still in the throes of a massive technological revolution, and we haven't fully integrated these changes into our classrooms yet. We know that technology has expanded our access to information and that it transformed instructional practices during the latter half of the twentieth century. We know it continues to change the way we live, work, and play. The introduction of educational technologies like computers, audiovisual aids, the Internet, and now AI has revolutionized (and is revolutionizing) teaching and learning methods. These innovations are supposed to improve the quality of education, revise curriculum standards, and enhance student learning. But have they? More on this in Chapter 2.

"Just Sit and Listen"

I don't know anyone who hasn't suffered some sort of microtrauma since COVID entered our lives. We're all shellshocked from the effects of the virus, not to mention the effects of climate change, the economy, and war.

We live in constant uncertainty. We may as well be on a different planet than the one I remember from a just couple of years ago.

Unfortunately, our education systems have been slow to catch up to this new reality, and a lot of current teaching practice would be more suited to a nineteenth or twentieth century classroom than our students of today.

I learned the secret to success in today's classrooms early, in second grade:

Miss B had given us a task to complete, and us seven-year-olds had questions. We all lined up at her desk, fidgety, chatty, and bored as she worked with each student. While watching Miss B, I caught on that she was displeased, and somehow, innately, I knew to sit cross-legged, my finger on my mouth and my hand held up, while my classmates continued to be what was considered unruly. She called out my exemplary behaviour to my classmates, and I got a gold star. The importance of this reward went above and beyond the glorious checkmarks that already littered my workbook pages: it meant *I mattered.*

Many generations have valued students' ability to sit still, concentrate, and focus on the task at hand. These skills made solid twentieth century factory workers who didn't question too much and produced with quiet efficiency. It also allowed teachers to have good "classroom management" — i.e., a controlled learning environment where they could deliver lessons without disruption or distraction. However, the notion that children learn better when they sit squirm-free for long periods of time has long since been disproven, and we now know accept the general rule that a child can sit still for about one minute per every year of age. Indeed, my second grade peers probably sat for seven minutes before giving up on pleasing Miss B.

Excitement, worry, and anxiety are common emotions that steal from stillness; sometimes, trouble focusing and hyperactivity are the culprits.

Regardless, we know that kids just aren't wired to sit still for long periods of time. Traditional (rote based) learning relied heavily on students simply listening to what was being said, but we also have four other senses that we can tap into to enrich our experience of the world. Our learning and understanding become much more meaningful and comprehensive when as many senses as possible are activated. This means children, contrary to sitting still, need to get out of their chairs; to touch, see, feel, smell, and taste; to fully synthesize what they are learning so that it makes sense to them in memorable, connected ways. A quiet classroom environment like Miss B's makes me uncomfortable. An out-of-control classroom with kids flying off their desks also makes me uncomfortable. What we're after is a hum of kids buzzing and sharing, walking around freely to explore, without feeling restricted or fearful of reprimand.

I learned this during a visit to a school, where I had the opportunity to observe an innovative teaching practice that included an arts component:

The teacher read a story to introduce the lesson, and the fourth grade class gathered around to act it out and discuss it. While this was going on, one boy left the group and meandered over to the small library near where I sat watching. I was surprised that this didn't register with the teacher. Instead, they just continued, and none of the other kids even noticed or paid any mind to the fact that he had walked off. So, I asked him, "Hi there, friend. What are you doing?"

"I'm getting a book," he replied. He looked at me as if I had four heads. Wasn't it obvious? He then had the option to rejoin the group, sit on a yoga ball, return to his desk, get a snack, or sign out to go to the bathroom, all without asking.

This kid had *options*. And by the way, the book he'd chosen was about the topic the class was discussing. He was very much alert and engaged.

Keeping in mind the fact that we certainly have to keep our kids safe above all else (and our little ones need more attention than our big kids in this respect), this setup felt dreamy for the teacher in me. It was also a direct contrast to my experience with another young student in another school far away, who'd had us clearing the entire class out the library because he was literally throwing tables around.

Conclusion: School Sucks

Now, you have some rudimentary background information that can help you understand why teachers teach the way they do and on which you can base or shape important preliminary conversations with your children's teachers to ensure your child's needs are being met.

There's a proverb that goes something like, "Show me who your friends are, and I'll tell you who you are." Basically, it means that each person's behaviour averages that of the five people who are closest to them in their life; that people end up absorbing the thoughts, behaviours, and values of those they surround themselves with. This in mind: remember how much time we said kids spend in school? Clearly, teachers are going to have a huge and powerful influence on their students!

The fact is, sometimes, teachers do need students to "just sit and listen". It's *how* they get them to do this that has to be revisited. I used to stop, stand still, and hum, and then wait. In a short time, I had the entire class humming with me. One voice brought the class back together.

What's important is to know as much as you can about the kind of teacher and type of classroom your child will spend those fourteen thousand and forty hours with. Most educators enter the profession because they love children, but they're not perfect, and part and parcel of the profession is the fact that teachers must continue learning throughout their career. Get to know their values toward, beliefs about, and approach to teaching. Your kid's experience in their classroom depends on it.

Teacher Talk Tips

Parents should ask their child's teacher:

- What is the basis for your approach to teaching?
- How do you address the whole child in your teaching practice, including in cognitive, physical, social, emotional, and creative capacities?
- How do you set up your class?
- Does your classroom environment encourage students to explore their passions?
- What strategies do you use to settle your class?
- Do you allow short breaks during class?
- Are there designated peace zones in your classroom where kids can decompress, deregulate, and take a moment to relax their minds?
- Do you incorporate varied modes of teaching delivery that call to all learners, beyond just auditory learners? Do you have visual prompts? Kinesthetic? Sensory?

Parents should think about:

- What the vibe of the classroom is. Does it feel safe? Respectful? Ask your child first.
- Whether they would want to be in that classroom all day.
- How all these things affect their child. Where are the gaps (if there are any)? What does your child need? Is the teacher's teaching style a good fit for your little genius?
- Whether your child has opportunities to use their body in fun ways.

Consider your child's needs:

- What are their interests?
- Do they need to be at the front of the classroom, near the teacher?
- Do they like to be called on, or do they prefer more one-to-one time with the teacher?
- Is there ample opportunity for the teacher to check in with your child periodically? How do they do this?
- What kind of validation do they need to learn and grow?
- Are there leadership opportunities for them?
- What are some physical activities you can do with them? Walking? Dancing? Singing?

Let's take my experience as a student in Mr. H's classroom as an example of how we can listen and learn from each other, and then I'll tell you the wonderful thing that happened by the end of my teaching practicum:

Remember I said earlier that this classroom made me anxious and uncomfortable? That's some of the questions in the previous lists answered right there.

Viewing the situation through my judgemental, uninformed lens, I initially assumed that Mr. H was an ineffective, uncaring teacher and that he treated the kids unkindly. The students sat in rows. He taught by textbook. His teaching methodology was what is referred to as the traditional "sage on the stage" approach, or teacher-centred education (we can't blame him; that's simply what we were taught in teachers' college). According to this methodology, the teacher is the holder of all knowledge and imparts it in a one-way communication model, where students take notes and then regurgitate this information back on a test, with very little or no feedback. It's passive and not very fascinating for kids, but some teachers still practice it.

Mr. H came from a country where teaching was one of the most

27

respected professions. He was very conservative and a perfect sage on the stage. He had a tough time understanding why education wasn't revered and respected by his students. So, he yelled at them: "You don't want to learn!"

Ouch. I shouldn't have been surprised when one of the student ringleaders, "D" (you'll remember him from before), said to me, "School sucks, Miss, but you make it fun." I had the experience and maturity to navigate the terrain for myself, and in the absence of an environment that allowed me to be my best self and that set me up to teach the way I knew I needed to, I had to create one that also ended up working well with the kids. Twelve-year-old "D" could not do this on his own.

As a parent, you can and should step up for your child. Approach teachers with an open heart and an open mind.

I learned that Mr. H was deeply sensitive and wanted the best for those kids, and we ended up learning from each other. Yes, school should be fun, as long as learning is happening. I needed to learn structure and strategies (to ensure curricular outcomes were being met); and to understand how important it was to hold space for the emerging citizens of our communities; to teach them that they can achieve their goals and reach their full potential. Mr. H taught me those things.

Over the three months I spent in his classroom, I watched Mr. H put hours into creating his lessons. I saw how he gave up his lunch hour to help kids that weren't his own students learn better reading strategies. He then sat at his desk and took time to meditate and reflect on how he could do better. I admired him, but realized all I could do was be true to myself. His teaching style was simply not a good fit for me. Ultimately, however, through our work together, he became kinder and softer to the kids, and I became more centered and focused on my deliverables.

Understand where your child's teacher is coming from, and don't make assumptions about them or why they teach the way they do. Start with compassion and questions and help them understand your child better. Show up. No one knows your child better than you do.

Mr. H gave me straight A's at the end of my term in his classroom, and I gave him a tiny Buddha to keep on his desk when I moved on to my second teaching practicum. Thank you, good sir.

2

ENTER, TECHNOLOGY

I HAD A BIG "A-HA!" moment when my daughter was nine.

One sunny summer afternoon, I sat and smacked keys on my keyboard in my capacity as Professional Email Returner (the title my daughter had given me to describe my job). It was a pleasant, ordinary day, and she was practicing cartwheels on our lawn with her friends. After a few minutes of this activity which I encouraged and applauded, she came back in, took a seat at her desk just across from my home office, opened up her tablet, and disappeared into Internet land.

"Lulu! Why aren't you outside with your friends? Get off that device and go play."

"But Mommy, I did enough cartwheels!"

I saw she was scribbling in a little notebook. Curious, just as I had been with the fourth grade little boy who'd wandered over to the class library, I simply asked, "What are you doing?"

I wasn't prepared for the answer. "I'm looking up the difference between Greek and Roman goddesses and copying my favourite ones in my book."

Holy moly. What could I say to that? "Carry on!"

I do believe that with the right circumstances and environment, all nine-year-olds can have the curiosity and ability to self-direct that my daughter continues to have to this day. Of course, there must be limits around how much time children spend clicking around, and they must have supervision around what sites they are visiting. They need time to slow down, exercise, get sunshine, learn how to form healthy relationships with others, scrape knees, muse, and be bored. These are some of the things that make and keep us human. Still, the machines are here, like it or not.

We are bombarded with and have access to enormous amounts of information, any time, plated and served to us on various devices. There is so much debate about this prevalence of technology, but I think it's probably fair to say that most believe it's a source of evil in the classroom and that it's harming our children. No one wants numbed, distracted, stressed out kids staring at screens, playing games, or consuming harmful content that interferes with development and mental health. We need to be hyperaware of how our kids are interfacing with tech and the harmful effects it can have. Some of these are:

- Obesity and related health problems, caused by lack of physical activity.
- Sleep disturbances, caused by excessive exposure to screens (especially before bedtime) which can interfere with sleep patterns.
- Stress and anxiety, caused by cyberbullying, and stress, caused by kids feeling that social media likes and followers give them "cred".
- Social isolation and impaired communication skills, caused by reduced face to face interactions and overreliance on digital communication.
- Addiction to and dependence on video games and tech for sources of entertainment.
- Privacy and cybersecurity risks kids don't understand.
- Consumption of inaccurate or inappropriate content.

That's one scary list that makes me want to take all our children and set them free in a disconnected, peaceful forest where all we have to worry about is the possibility of a broken limb and maybe—God forbid—a wild animal attacking them, like in the good old days. Then again, that mindset in itself represents a polarity. We need to find a safe, middle-of-the-road way to exist in this hyped-up world, and we need to teach kids the skills they will need if they are to be aware of, never mind survive, digital threats. We need to teach them how to thrive, even though we are still trying to figure it out ourselves.

There are ways in which tech has already transformed the classroom when used appropriately which we need to understand. So that we can also understand the more positive impacts of this transformation, here's another, less terrifying list, this time of the *advantages* presented by tech. There are some strange educational and "tech speak" words you may not have heard before, so please go have a look at the Glossary at the end of this book for definitions, if need be.

- Access to information and digital resources like libraries and eBooks, allowing students to explore and research goddesses (or other things that interest them).
- Educational apps, interactive software, multimedia presentations, and gaming and virtual labs that can be used in the classroom to mirror what's used outside in the real world, allowing teachers to explain concepts in various dynamic, visually appealing ways.
- Personalized learning, data analytics, and flexible learning paths, allowing teachers to more easily create and provide customized content tailored to individual student needs.
- Collaboration and communication platforms, allowing students the opportunity to work together, share ideas, and provide feedback. Email, messaging apps, or online portals also allow teachers to communicate with students and parents more efficiently.

- The seamless development of digital literacy, critical thinking, and problem-solving skills that kids will need as they navigate the digital world and workplace.
- The option of remote learning for students who cannot be physically present at school, or who face geographical challenges related to getting to school.
- Accessibility. This is a big one. There are so many amazing tools, apps, and platforms that have leveled the playing field in the classroom for kids who need support. Please flip right to the Glossary for more information on this one.

Maybe we can settle down a bit and recognize that, when used appropriately, digital learning provides a lot of benefits to students. Still, this list might do little to appease your worries, if they go deep enough.

AI: Will It Kill Us?

Computers and cellphones haven't killed us, but some believe artificial intelligence (AI) might. It's revolutionary, and it's on everyone's mind, one way or another. Education thought leaders and doers are trying to figure out how massive databases or large language models (LLMs) like ChatGPT's GPT-4, Google Gemini, or Facebook LLaMa will impact how kids learn and do assignments, and how they are assessed.

Before we get any more intimidated and confused by this strange language and its implications, let's look at what AI is and what it is not.

AI is a branch of computer science that can carry out tasks that some think only humans could and should do. It develops algorithms and technologies that enable machines to perform tasks which typically require human intelligence, like problem-solving, pattern recognition, understanding natural language, and decision-making. It has the capacity to carry out tasks that humans find tedious and monotonous (like my lists in this chapter and the Glossary, for example), analyze enormous datasets, and find patterns with lightning speed. Furthermore, AI makes decisions based on this data.

What AI does *not* do is reason like a human does. Instead, it operates based on the information and rules of logic it has been provided with.

Perhaps our problem is that we believe AI differs from computers. When they were first introduced to the general public, we thought computers were going to be the end of us, too, but if you think about it, a computer still needs humans to tell it what to do. Many of us think that AI doesn't need us — that it can do what it likes — but right now, this is untrue, because it isn't self aware. HAL-9000, the evil AI in Arthur C. Clarke's *Space Odyssey* series (adapted brilliantly for the screen by Stanley Kubrick in *2001: A Space Odyssey*), planted the seed of AI having the potential to overtake humanity in the public's mind, but the ominous behaviour of HAL-9000 still only sits in the realm of science fiction and pop culture today.

Here's an overly simplified example of how AI — specifically, ChatGPT — might work. It's important we understand this, because it's freaking teachers out and is already affecting how your kids do school:

First, think of a subject that interests you. This could be grasshoppers, cars, tomato sauce... anything random. Now imagine an entire library of information, or data, about that one subject floating all over the Internet. Imagine that you want specific information, presented to you in a certain way (the rules), about that subject. Let's look at tomato sauce, for example. I typed into the ChatGPT prompt bar, "Write me an essay on the history of tomato sauce." You know what it pumped out? *The Culinary Odyssey: A Journey Through the History of Tomato Sauce*, a whole essay that included information about the origin of tomato sauce, its evolution in Europe, and tomato sauce in contemporary cuisine.

Questions (or prompts, as they are called in the AI world) can be very detailed and structured, and often include an intended outcome. This means we can prompt it to write that tomato sauce essay in Shakespearean language (see Appendix A for the full essays). Depending on how good your prompt is, you can get a whole bunch of cool information curated just for you, but the rules (and thus the outputs generated) are still up to us humanoids.

Well, that's it. Kids don't have to do anything anymore besides type in a prompt or two.

Or do they?

AI: Will It Make Our Kids Lazy?

We have an ethical dilemma on our hands when it comes to the use of AI, and need to be very careful with how we consume and use the content it generates. LLMs scrape information from the Internet and publicly available sources, so users run the risk of unintentionally pulling the copyrighted and intellectual property of others without even knowing. And you know what else? AI is susceptible to producing completely inaccurate, incorrect, or nonsensical outputs, called AI hallucinations. The details in the tomato sauce essay may not even be true.

There's a lot of gunk in cyberspace, so we can't rely solely on AI-generated content. High quality data is a must, as are solid rules to define a clear purpose for using AI. Most importantly, a human eye is required, to ensure trusted sources are checked and verified (so that output is authentic). Sources must always be scrubbed.

We're part of the way there, but we have work to do. We've come up with AI detectors (tools that can tell if AI is generating content). Teachers use Turnitin, for example, an AI writing detection tool used to scour student work and ensure it's original. However, AI is getting more and more sophisticated, and we need to work on parameters around it so that we harness the power of this new technology in respectful ways, so that we use it for good, not to cheat or take shortcuts.

At this moment, we are figuring out how AI will become part of our day to day lives. Trailblazers like Sam Ransbotham (professor of analytics at the Carroll School of Management at Boston College and guest editor for MIT Sloan Management Review's Artificial Intelligence and Business Strategy Big Ideas initiative) tell us it won't be AI that takes our jobs, but other humans who know how to use it. They also say that if the organizations we're working for today aren't currently using AI, they're the ones that are going to go out of business.[1] Even still, the unknown is unsettling, and parents worry that overreliance on technology (and specifically AI) in all areas of their children's lives will diminish their cognitive skills. How will they learn to think? Write? Do math? How are we preparing them for the futures?

Just a few years ago, it was considered outrageous to have a computer in the classroom. In the early 2000s, I was called in by the administration of a school for bringing in my own personal laptop and projecting images to show the third graders I was teaching the difference between a city and a town for our social studies class. You can likewise imagine the response I got when I had the audacity to ask for a hardwire connection to the Internet!

Think of that scenario today. It's not so scandalous anymore, right? School staff and students have integrated devices into learning and teaching in varying degrees all over the world. However, I don't think we've done this as effectively as we had anticipated yet.

Sometimes, it is appropriate for teachers to shift their pedagogy to

---

[1] GBH Forum Network (2024). Sourced from @gbhforumnetwork on Instagram Reels.

incorporate technology. Other times, it's not. A nature walk designed to develop students' observational skills and appreciation for the natural world is a nice example of an activity where technology is not applicable. All the kids need are their eyes and body, and maybe a magnifying glass. When they are *back* in the classroom, however, they could use some form of tech to categorize, graph, or write about the specimens they have collected or observed.

Data Tells a Story

We now have data that illustrates the impact of the influx of technology in our children's lives. Since 2003, Giancarlo Brotto of Pave Edu Inc., Canada, a worldwide education thinker and leader, has been watching, gathering, and analysing trends from PISA (Programme for International Student Assessment), a worldwide study conducted annually by the OECD (Organisation for Economic Co-operation and Development) that measures fifteen-year-old students' performance in mathematics, science, and reading literacy. The report gives policymakers insight into trends and the effectiveness of educational systems across countries and regions, so it's a pretty big deal, and of course, every country wants to sit at number one on the report. Where does your country rank? You can see at www.oecd.org.

Mr. Brotto focused his analysis on mathematics—specifically, the relationship between student performance in math and the amount of time students spent on devices at school. He's taken the PISA data and made it a little less daunting for the general public to understand. The graph you'll look at in a moment shows us this relationship between student device usage and different countries' scores. You'll notice that Japan, which landed at number one for student achievement in mathematics in 2003, had the second lowest frequency of computer use by students at school.

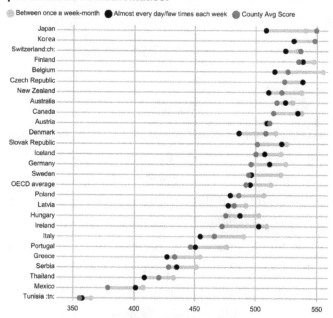

2003 Frequency of computer use at school and student performance in mathematics.

○ Between once a week-month ● Almost every day/few times each week ● County Avg Score

Chart: Pave Edu Inc. * Source: OECD, PISA 203 Database, Table 4.4 . Created with Datawrapper

Now, let's look at 2022:

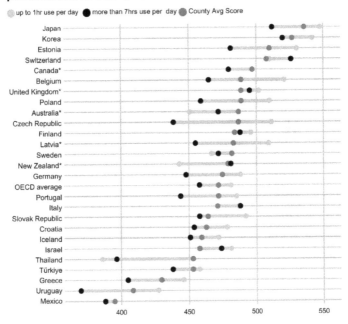

2022 Frequency of device use at school and student performance in mathematics

up to 1hr use per day ● more than 7hrs use per day County Avg Score

Differences between categroies are statistically significant (see PISA Results Volume I Anex A3)
Chart: Pave Edu Inc. - Source: OECD, PISA 2022 Database, Volune I Annex 9 Chapter 5 Created with Datawrapper

In 2022, student usage increased and scores stayed low. Usage at one hour a day resulted in slightly better scores. The higher frequency of computer use at school has not led to higher student performance. In fact, the opposite is true: in most countries, students who reportedly used technology the most in learning environments generally performed worse on international assessments.

The latest 2023 PISA report reiterates this:

> *The use of digital devices in schools is a contentious issue in many countries. While PISA shows a positive relationship between the*

intentional integration of technology in school education and student performance, devices used for leisure such as smartphones can distract from learning, expose students to cyber bullying and compromise their privacy. They are also highly addictive. On average across OECD countries, 45% of students reported feeling nervous or anxious if their phones were not near them.

The use of phones and other digital devices can also impact classroom learning. On average across OECD countries, 65% of students reported being distracted by using digital devices in at least some maths lessons. The proportion topped 80% in Argentina, Brazil, Canada, Chile, Finland, Latvia, Mongolia, New Zealand and Uruguay. Just as importantly, across the OECD, 59% of students said their attention was diverted due to other students using phones, tablets or laptops in at least some maths lessons. Interestingly, only 18% of students in Japan and 32% in Korea reported this level of distraction.[2]

But wait. There are a few more numbers we can consider here. Common Sense Media, a nonprofit organization dedicated to helping families and educators navigate the digital world safely and responsibly, has captured data to reflect our children's "media diet". Here's the landscape usage for teens in 2015:

- *Passive Consumption: Thirty-nine percent listening to music, watching videos, watching TV, and reading.*
- *Interactive Consumption: Twenty-five percent playing games and browsing websites.*
- *Communication: Twenty-six percent using social media and*

---

[2] Schleicher, A. (2022); *PISA 2022 Insights and Interpretations*. OECD (p. 33) (www.oecd.org/pisa).

40

video chatting.

- *Creation: Three percent making art, composing music, writing, and programming.*

Access and usage have increased, according to their latest 2019 report. Other than that, not much else has changed.[3] We can see that our kids' media diets are heavy with passive and interactive consumption, with very little time dedicated to creation. I'd like to think that creation might be behind PISA's note on "intentional integration of technology in school education" quoted above. Either way, this sure isn't happening in our schools yet.

Remember my initial response to Lulu when she swapped cartwheeling for screen time? ("Get off that device!") I'd assumed my daughter was using her device passively, in a way that wasn't activating her brain (just like the data suggests). But she wasn't. She was *creating* something very personal to her (the goddess list) and she was *learning*. This is the ticket!

Kids aren't thinking when they're ogling at their screens. They aren't producing, crafting, designing, forming, making, or developing anything. Educators must therefore reflect deeply on how any technology can support thinking and doing in our schools, and parents must limit activities that are purely consumptive or inappropriate at home.

Here are some guidelines to keep screen time in check, according to age:[4]

- Children aged two and under: No screen time.
- Children aged two to four: Less than one hour a day.
- Children aged five to seventeen: Maximum of two hours a day.

---

[3] Please see www.commonsensemedia.org/media-use-by-tweens-and-teens-2019-infographic

[4] Based on AboutKidsHealth (2020): *Screen time: Overview* (www.aboutkidshealth.ca/screen-time-overview).

Together, we must create more mindful and balanced digital habits for our kids. This starts with us understanding how they are currently using their devices, both in and out of school.

At home, parents have the power to set boundaries, and there are tools out there to help you better understand and manage device usage and your children's screen time. See Appendix B for a range of features to help you manage screen time, enforce digital parameters for screen usage, and promote healthy online habits for both children and adults. Please explore these options to find the app that best suits your needs and preferences.

One more tip: You can shut it all down at a certain time every day. Service providers offer wireless modems that allow you to restrict access or set time limits for Internet usage. Think of the "lights out" rule for bedtime and apply the same principle to Internet use.

Pay attention to what your kids are doing online, dear parents. It's critical. Just like too much sugar and some of the chemicals in our food, it can make them sick if not handled with care. You're not going to stop your kids from eating altogether, but you are going to pay attention to the quality of their diets. Much the same attitude is needed for technology use.

Technology and Children's Mental Health

Is there anyone out there who isn't concerned about the potential impact of technology on their child's mental health these days?

When I was growing up, my parents' biggest fears for me were teenage pregnancy and alcohol and drug use. Today, we worry about a whole host of mental illness in addition to these things. It's a tough time to be a parent.

There's no doubt about it: technology usage affects mental health and wellbeing. Recall that cyberbullying, social isolation, sleep deprivation, and harmful content (common side effects of inappropriate or excessive use of technology) are all potential contributors to poor childhood mental health. There's another one that is also a biggie: comparison and unrealistic standards.

We know that social media platforms often portray idealized or curated versions of life. Constant exposure to such unattainable standards of beauty and lifestyle can lead kids to believe they are somehow lacking in comparison to their peers. It can exacerbate mental health issues and even contribute to the prevalence of suicidal ideation. This is scary and heartbreaking. Every child is different, so some emerge relatively unscathed; others do not.

It's not only your kids' screen use that impacts their mental health, too; it's *your* screen use. "I'll be right there!" "Just one more email!" I said these things many times when Lulu was little and calling for me.

It's neither possible nor healthy for parents to meet every single need children have. We can't be there every second of the day. In fact, they wouldn't thrive if we could. What we *can* do is spend as much time as possible with our kids, and what is equally important to this is *how* we show up. The greatest gift parents can give to their children is absolute presence of mind. If we can let everything fall away and truly pay attention with our whole being when we are with our kids, listening with our hearts and minds, we can catch them when they fall and need a safe place to land during times of struggle.

At times, children aren't quite sure how to tell us what they need, even if it's just a hug. If we're drafting that last email in our heads while they're telling us about their troubles, they'll pick up on this, and won't attempt to unload whatever it is they need to in the future. When parents are chronically unavailable, things can get concerning, and children may look for validation in unhealthy places.

I'm not saying it is easy to be fully present with your kids. It takes practice, awareness, patience, the ability to self-reflect on our own behaviours, and a heap of love. Pause, sit with and collect yourself for even a minute, and breathe to shut off all the noise surrounding you. This simple exercise can help you better navigate situations and respond appropriately.

Once this foundation is in place, your kids can learn healthy strategies to navigate bullies, criticism, and failure. They can develop grit, perseverance, and determination. Carol Dweck, a prominent psychologist and a Lewis Virginia Eaton Professor of Psychology at Stanford University, is best known for her book *Mindset: The New Psychology of Success.*[5] Her research on motivation, achievement, and mindset theory explores the concept of a "growth mindset" versus a "fixed mindset". Here's the difference, according to Dr. Dweck:

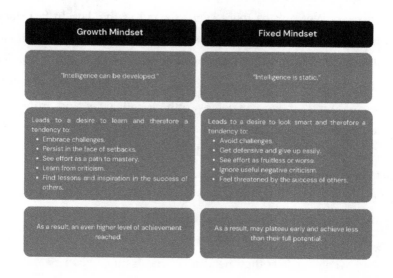

---

[5] Dweck, C. (2008): *Mindset: The New Psychology of Success*. New York, USA: Ballantine Books.

HOW TO TALK TO TEACHERS

The goal is to get kids in the "growth mindset" zone and stay there, to keep mental health in check.

This can be taught. While growth mindset principles may not be explicitly outlined in your child's curriculum, educators can integrate these concepts into their teaching practice, to support student learning and wellbeing. Teachers can encourage effort, adaptability, a positive environment, and a love of learning to help students develop the skills and the attitudes needed for success in school and beyond.

Both my husband and I work in the tech industry. As such, we have a good understanding and insight into tech trends and online safety to protect our daughter and have taught her how to protect herself. That spectacular little girl who was cataloguing Aphrodite and Venus in her notebook is now a wise young lady, and she's nailing it. When I asked Lulu for her perspective on assistive AI technology like ChatGPT, she said, "You can use it to get ideas, but you can't just copy-and-paste what it gives you. You have to check it for bias and truth, and you have to include your own voice. ChatGPT has no soul, and writing is all about the soul."

Mic drop.

Conclusion: Enter, Technology

There are many occasions now where kids know more about technology than their teachers, and this can be daunting for educators. They are literally learning on the fly, alongside their students. I don't think teaching has ever been so stressful, given the large class sizes, lack of resources and support, out-of-this-world technology, and sheer number of unhappy, unhealthy students.

Some educators embrace teaching with technology and are willing to try new approaches. Some aren't comfortable with it all. Most lie somewhere in the middle. This means that there are inconsistencies in terms of how lessons are delivered from school year to school year, and sadly, this affects the students. Much depends on whether your child wins what I call the "teacher lottery" and which class they land in at the beginning of each school year.

Still, parents aren't helpless to improve their kids' learning outcomes and ensure their kids are healthy, physically, and mentally. Get to know where your kids' teachers sit on their own learning journey and how their pedagogy has (or has not) been affected by technology.

Be fully present when you're with your child and be on the lookout for any behaviour that is out of the ordinary. Seeking assistance for children facing mental health challenges is essential. Reach out for support from qualified professionals and access appropriate resources and guidance to address your child's mental health (if necessary), so they can thrive and overcome challenges with appropriate care and intervention.

Technology isn't a quick fix, and it can be detrimental to kids' health and wellbeing. As we've established, some lessons are taught better without it. I'm with Alvin Toffler — a prominent American writer, futurist, and social critic known for his works on the impact of technological change on society — in this regard. In 1970, he wrote, "The illiterate of the twenty-first century will not be those who cannot read and write, but those who cannot learn, unlearn, and relearn."[6] This highlights the importance of adaptability and lifelong learning in the rapidly changing landscape of the twenty-first century.

My second-grade teacher Miss B wasn't all bad. I can spell, and anyway, if I do spell a word wrong, my computer program puts a red squiggly line under it for me, so I know to correct it. This technological intervention presents a new way for me to learn, and I think it's better than

---

[6] Toffler, A. (1970): *Future Shock*. New York: Random House (p. 367).

writing the word out ten times and handing it back to my teacher for a check mark.

I work differently with AI today than I did only two years ago, and I'm okay.

Teacher Talk Tips

Parents should ask their child's teacher:

- How do you use technology for learning?
- How is technology integrated mindfully into the curriculum?
- Can you tell me about any signs or behaviours you've noticed in my child that may indicate they're experiencing mental health challenges?
- How do you address social and emotional learning in your curriculum or classroom activities?
- What strategies do you use to support students who may be struggling with anxiety, depression, or other mental health issues?
- What steps can we take together to ensure that my child receives the support they need to thrive academically and emotionally in your classroom?

Parents should think about:

- Whether their child *consumes* technology or *interacts* with it to create and learn.
- Whether they have visibility into what their child is searching, and whether they have parameters in place to prevent their children from searching for unsavoury subjects.
- Whether they discuss what their child is searching, and why.
- Whether they have age-appropriate screentime limits in place.

- Whether they have the skills and ability to center themselves so they can be present with their child.

Consider also your child's needs:
- Does technology interfere with or support their learning?
- Are there applications, programs, or games that they use for educational purposes and that you can share with their teacher?
- Are there any changes in behaviour, sleep patterns, appetite, or attention span in them?
- Are there any changes in their academic performance or socialization at school?

I had a wonderful job in the Edtech industry for several years. I helped educators integrate technology in meaningful ways, and I also helped get lots and lots of sales for the products the company was selling. I loved that part of my career, because it gave me the opportunity to meet, collaborate with, and support some of the best teachers in Canada and the world. We created an incredible tribe that produced outstanding examples of teaching delivery and deep learning that was shared with others to leverage — wait for it! — *technology*. These innovators were fearless, testing and trying and failing and learning how we enhance learning using technology *without* jeopardizing our kids' wellbeing. Right now, they are the ones pioneering how we will and will not use AI in the classroom going forward.

There were solid, important lessons garnered from that time that still make sense to me today. Namely: tech can never replace strong teaching practices and must be used thoughtfully, mindfully, and with a clear purpose. Tech cannot replace a human teacher.

The introduction of tech into our world has been almost as cataclysmic as the discovery of fire was for our forebearers. Fire could have definitely hurt them, but it could also warm them and cook their food. We just need to keep asking each other the same question again and again, so none of us gets scorched: "What are we doing and why are we doing it?"

3

THEY CAN'T BE DOCTORS IF THEY CAN'T SPELL: ASSESSMENT AND THE GLOBAL COMPETENCIES FOR THE TWENTY-FIRST CENTURY

———

R EADIN', WRITIN', 'RITHMETIC. MANY WELL-MEANING parents firmly believe that the three Rs are necessary if we are to function successfully in society. And sure, in yesterday's world, they were enough, but if we can take anything away from the last chapter, it's that machines are radically changing how we get things done.

I admit, I have a real pet peeve about spelling and grammar crimes. They irk me to no end. Spellcheck and Grammarly (a free AI writing assistant that students often use) minimize these infractions in written work, which helps soothe my soul. This, however, begs the question of: if students no longer get gold stars for stellar spelling alone, what are the competencies they'll need in order to succeed when they enter the real world?

This makes me think of "S", a student I remember fondly because it broke my heart to see her struggle. I wanted to help her but was unable to, because the kind of help she needed would have been considered cheating at the time.

S was a bright, inquisitive third grade student whose family had just immigrated to Canada, into a wealthy monocultural community that wasn't her own. English was her second language, and she often felt deeply frustrated when she struggled to get her thoughts on paper. She didn't fully understand written instructions, and tests were not her thing. I'll never forget her face when, during an end-of-unit social science test, she came to my desk and asked I could tell her what to do: "Please, Miss, please?" I was in my second practicum in teachers' college with a new mentor, a by-the-book veteran teacher who ran a tight ship. Her students came into the grade writing their names, adding, and subtracting, and exited the grade writing paragraphs and doing fractions and long division. There was no messing around.

My hands were tied.

I could only reread the question to S and apologize for not being able to do more. She walked back to her desk in tears. There was no place in that test where S could show me what she knew in varied formats and be graded for how she could think.

Since then, we have realized that there is real diversity in how students learn, as well as how they can demonstrate their understanding and the progress they've made. We've had to adjust to give every child the opportunities they need to show mastery.

Later, I met "C", a nonverbal child on the autism spectrum, through an extraordinary Canadian teacher and leader, Mr. A. Mr. A shared that C struggled with repetition, as well as growing and shrinking pattern recognition. After a lot of time sitting with C one-to-one, Mr. A decided to try something different: a game-based platform where C could play with the problems. Mr. A felt C understood what they were being tasked with; they just couldn't express this understanding. And eureka! — Mr. A was right: C did understand. They just needed the right tools and form of assessment to show it in their own way.

Both S and C (and those like them) have the right to be honoured and respected and to show us their own authentic selves in their learning.

We'll do a deeper dive into assessment later in this chapter, but first, let's look at the shift in the skills we need to teach students to prepare them for life outside the safety of the classroom. After all, we have to understand what we are grading for before any work can be assessed.

You'll recall from Chapter 1 that memorizing facts, sitting still, nice spelling and grammar, knowing twelve multiplied by eight off the top of our heads, and acing the test were the keys to success for a long time. It's what we (us parents) were taught when we were in school, so, by default, it's what we expect from our kids. But today's world demands different, transferable competencies, and education systems have to integrate these into the curriculum.

Education leaders, policymakers, and thinkers have recognized this disconnect between what is happening in the classroom and the goings on outside the classroom after the bell rings. Today, the world is interdependent, interconnected, and changing at breakneck speed. As such, students need to be prepared for active participation in a global society. "Readin', writin', and 'rithmetic" are foundational to this, and the tech we now have helps with this, too, but we need to build on these competencies. The traditional academic knowledge that parents who attended school in the pre-Internet days still hold dear isn't enough anymore.

The global learning competencies were created to provide a framework to help students better prepare for a twenty-first-century world. International organizations like the United Nations Educational, Scientific and Cultural Organization (UNESCO), the Organization for Economic Cooperation and Development (OECD), and the Programme for

International Student Assessment (PISA), along with education leaders worldwide, have contributed to the development of a list detailing the skills, attitudes, and behaviours essential for kids to be prepared for successful, healthy adulting. In Canada, we've started with six new competencies that are slowly being woven into the curriculum. Here they are in another list. See Appendix C for deeper insight; it's pretty meaty stuff.

1. Critical thinking and problem-solving.
2. Innovation, creativity, and entrepreneurship.
3. Learning to learn/self-awareness and self-direction.
4. Collaboration, teamwork, and leadership.
5. Communication and language skills.
6. Global citizenship and sustainability.

Others have been added as we continue to evolve:

7. Cultural awareness and sensitivity.
8. Global citizenship and ethical responsibility.
9. Global and political awareness
10. Technical literacy.
11. Flexibility and adaptability.
12. Environmental sustainability.
13. Empathy and intercultural competence.

What a fantastic, holistic list. If each one is taught and modelled to children, we'll all get to witness and celebrate a fuller spectrum and expression of who each child is. I, however, have two competencies I'd add to bookend this list with: connection and contribution. I have respect and admiration for Joanne McEachen, another worldwide education leader who founded The Learner First,[7] and she taught me that we have to start with connection to the self first, then connection to others, then connection to humanity, so we can understand our purpose on this physical plane.

At the risk of getting a bit highbrow here, French philosopher René Descartes wrote the famous line, "I think, therefore I am," in his work *Meditations on First Philosophy*, published in 1641. We are sentient, thinking beings, and thus we exist. What niggles at me (and what I think matters most) is *how* we exist. Dare I update and add to the quote "I *connect*, therefore I am"?

It's a teacher's job to deliver lessons and present information in a way that engages students and infuses the whopping thirteen global learning competencies into their teaching practice (also known as pedagogy), and to support the synthesis of every child's learning. Overly simplified, this process might go something like this:

A student spells the word "cat" properly and can write about cats based on what their teacher has presented. That's nice. Well done.

And?

The student exhibits inquiry and extends their learning, and then maybe creates a cat not-for-profit to save strays.

Awesome!

The student has demonstrated, synthesized, and concretized "cat". They care about cats and have done something to help them. In doing so, they have met and collaborated with other cat-caring people. They've found purpose in "cat".

Bingo.

Connected people are happy people. In this vein, I find the rat park experiment conducted by psychologist Bruce K. Alexander and his

---

[7] Please see www.thelearnerfirst.com

colleagues in the 1970s fascinating.[8] The study's aim was to examine how environment and social factors play a part in addiction and drug use. Bruce K. Alexander challenged the traditional lab experiment on addiction, where rats were isolated in small cages with access to two water bottles (one with laced with cocaine or morphine, the other just good old H_2O). In these experiments, the poor beings consistently opted for the juiced-up water, and it was believed that the substance contributed to addiction. Our friend Bruce changed up this traditional model: he put the rats in a pleasant, stimulating, social environment. Rat friendships and communities formed. The rats connected! With this connection came a decreased preference for the "drug" water.

We're not rats, but we do need each other for our wellbeing. We know that happy, healthy, connected kids whose needs are met generally do better in life. Abraham Maslow said so (he's in the Glossary; look him up). He was instrumental to our understanding of human behaviour (we have to give him props for that). When we reach a point where we are all confident that our school systems help develop connected kids, our teachers can then work to help students find their purpose.

This is a lifelong journey, with many trials and tribulations, but school can be a place where children safely explore and express who they are. To circle back to the cats example we used earlier, our sample student could think and know a whole lot about cats, but it is by taking action and connecting with others, with purpose and intent to help, that the student's spirit comes alive.

All of this in mind, let's get into grades (this is where it gets funky).

---

[8] Hadaway, P.F.; Alexander, B.K.; Coambs, R.B.; Beyerstein, B. (1979): *The effect of housing and gender on preference for morphine-sucrose solutions in rats.* Psychopharmacology. 66 (1): 87–91.

Nothing Less Than One Hundred Percent

My dad was a passionate, determined, tenacious, really smart man who I admired and respected. I learned a lot from him and marveled at how he, along with his brothers, became a successful entrepreneur, even though he had had no more than a first grade education.

He had high expectations of me, and if I came home with ninety-nine percent on a test, I knew I'd be met with, "Why not one hundred percent?" A lot of parents are over-the-top-intense about their children's grades, and the resulting pressure we put on our kids can be excruciating. We push them because we believe good marks in school mean they've done a good job and they'll be rewarded with security and stability. We don't want to harm our children; we just want what we think is best for them.

We're familiar with formative assessments, like the test my dear little S was trying to complete at the beginning of this chapter. I knew S had a good grasp on the content — she knew the answers — but unfortunately, the written test was the only chance she had to show her chops, and the C she got didn't reflected her capabilities.

S would be assessed differently today, because aside from the test, her teacher could collect varied modes of assessment to produce a final mark. Besides the test (which is, for some students, a good indicator of how successfully instruction was received), here are some different methods teachers can employ that allow students with diverse strengths to exhibit their thinking and showcase their learning:

- Project-based assignments (more on this later).
- Portfolios (a long-term collection of student output and evidence of learning).
- Anecdotal tests (observation in scenarios where students are practicing a skill).

- Peer and self assessment (when students review their own work and the work of their classmates).
- Multimedia presentations (podcasts, slides, videos, and so on).
- Arts-based projects (songs, dances, poems, and so on).

The way we currently assess students is, we start with knowledge and add in thinking, application, communication, and all the global competencies. We bundle them all together, and *then* pull together a mark. However, assessment remains sticky. Educators have to be fair, clear, and, most of all, free of bias. They can provide rubrics, for example, to explain the expectations and performance levels and describe how student output is evaluated, to provide a more accurate understanding of the grade. Rubrics allow for feedback, so students can course correct and improve. Because of this, rubrics are far gentler than a bold red number or letter planted in the at top-right-hand corner of a test that tells a student they are either a failure or a superstar (have a peek at Appendix D for an example of a rubric that you can play with). With these approaches, perhaps my little student S would have received at least a B+/Level 3+, which is what I think she truly deserved. Maybe her self-esteem would have been left intact.

It would be all well and good for me to propose we base our assessments on rubrics alone and ditch grades entirely, but let's be real: we are in transition right now. If your child wants to be a doctor, for example, good grades still dictate their entrance into postsecondary education and competitive medical schools. Until we get our approach to assessment right and change our beliefs that an A/Level 4 inherently defines who our children are and the success they'll have in their careers, parents will (inevitably) continue to push students to "play the game", like I and some of you out there did when in school, with success. I remember using those exact words with Lulu ("play the game") when she was in first grade and she asked me what her scores meant: "Just get good grades, Lulu. Play the game." In the end, the only reason she started caring about getting outstanding grades was because her parents did. We were teaching her to emphasize her marks, and in so doing, we were also teaching her that if she did, she was "good" in our minds.

We realized this sooner or later and decided to do things a little differently in our house, and we were very successful. If Lulu came home with a grade she was unhappy with, we never, ever shamed or judged her. We didn't want to lead her to believe that her value was based on a grade. We gave her the space to think about what had happened, and when she was ready, we asked the following questions:

1. How do feel about your grade?
2. What grade do you want?
3. What are you going to do differently to achieve the grade you want?
4. What tools or help do you need from us to reach your goal? From your teacher? From others?

Our job as parents was to listen and guide. We wanted to do everything in our power to get her a better grade, but it was Lulu who needed to put the effort in. She needed to do the work to achieve her goals. It was up to us to help her find the tactics and support she would need to be successful in this journey. The *tactics* used here (not the results) are what is important, because they become meaningful life skills that can be applied to any challenge our children may face throughout their lives. We focused on how she could move the needle, not the marks themselves.

I've asked Lulu if I can share the following example to demonstrate, and she's okay with it:

She once received a fifty-four percent on her first chemistry test of the year. She was disappointed, discouraged, and anxious, because she knew that to stay in her program, the minimum was a seventy-five percent overall grade for this course. She got extra help by asking her teacher for examples of what she was learning over and above what was being provided in class. She went online and found videos. She worked with a friend. In summary, she found the tactics, worked hard, and put in the effort. She came out with seventy-eight percent by the end of the school year.

Here's the kicker: we didn't focus on the numerical grade. It didn't matter where she started or where she ended up. We focused on the *jump* she made from fifty-four percent to seventy-eight percent.

How do you define that? I call it growth. We taught her to practice a *growth mindset* (we spoke about this in our last chapter).

None of this works in the absence of one thing: motivation. We still need to be careful with this, though: if we think about it logically, it can't be healthy for a child to only be motivated to do well in school because they feel that, at some level, their parents' love and acceptance is contingent on them getting the grade that has been imposed on them by their parents. My father set one hundred percent as my goal, not me, and I accepted this as the only acceptable result solely because I didn't want to disappoint him. This was unsustainable.

Sometimes, kids don't seem to be motivated by anything. Then what?

This situation then becomes a question of why. Lack of self-esteem can be a contributor, as can fear and shame — or maybe they just don't know what motivates them and some exploration is required. Remember, there is help out there if your child needs it. Your child's wellbeing is most important.

Our approach with Lulu has been very effective. Lulu became highly motivated to stay in her program and she worked hard to make sure she did, not because we wanted her to, but because *she* wanted to. But things don't always work out the way we like, right? Well, if Lulu hadn't achieved the "right" marks to continue on the path she'd chosen, we would have helped her navigate that, too, teaching her flexibility and agility in the process. She knows that challenges and setbacks are part of the package we call life. Without them, we can't grow, but we *can* choose to face them without suffering and struggle. I think that's healthy.

We give our daughter the latitude to decide what marks she wants, and accept her decisions. Full transparency (guilty as charged): there have been times when her grade has been satisfactory to her but we secretly wanted her to do better. However, we learned that it was more important that we respect her choices so she could feel independent and empowered, rather than pushing

Sound crazy? It works. Lulu continues to hustle and thrive today. She's not the perfect child (that would be boring) and we're not the perfect parents (we make mistakes like everyone else). Our focus is to be right there when our daughter stumbles. We officiate if we need to, but Lulu is learning to play her own game, by her own rules.

School Isn't Always for Everyone... But It Can Be: Skilled Trades and Artists

Skilled Trades

When I went to high school (a period Lulu calls "the dawn of time"), students were streamed into different pathways depending on their marks. "Academic" kids went to one school while "technical" kids went to another. This pitted the "smart" kids who figured out how to write a test with success against the "dumb" kids who did not score so well. Thankfully, there has been some work done to end this practice in Lulu's world, but sadly, many of these fundamental attitudes remain. While the academic kids who can play that game I keep referring to and get those

A's double down on research, writing, thinking, strong oral communication, and problem-solving, the technical kids drill down on hands-on experience, technical communication, industry-specific knowledge, and problem-solving in the context of the career they are pursuing.

A dear lifelong friend of mine is a master tradesperson. I don't think there's anything he can't figure out how to build or fix. "R" has so many skills and so much knowledge that to watch him create is captivating. However, his abilities have not always been appreciated by the people he serves. He tells me that most often, he will walk into a prospective job and be met with assumptions about his intelligence. I recall one instance he shared where his client, nostrils flaring, gave him instructions in very simple language (as if speaking to a child) on "how he was to behave on the property", where he could and could not put his materials, where he could and could not use the bathroom, where he could and could not eat... you get the picture.

R decided to go to teachers' college, believing that a degree would give him credibility and validate his work. Turns out that while R has the innate ability, compassion, and kindness to teach, it just isn't his calling. He only wanted to go to teachers' college so he would not be called "dirty" or be disrespected because of his profession. He thought that a degree would change the beliefs of some people who assumed that because he worked with his hands, he had no smarts.

R got that certificate. However, just like the Scarecrow in *The Wizard of Oz*, a piece of paper didn't prove that R was intelligent, and he learned that those who truly saw and appreciated his talent were the only ones who mattered.

Not many know he is a certified teacher today. I wonder where he keeps his degree. I'm pretty sure it's not in his toolbox! Yet that piece of paper holds real power and status in society.

Professionals are "white collar", and their professions are considered to be "clean". Most parents want their kids to become doctors or professionals, and in that wish, they fail to understand or acknowledge the value of a skills-based education and career. We need the trades, and the talents and abilities of tradespeople must be respected. Period.

When industrialization took over, vocational education became more and more important, and schools began to offer specialized training to prepare students for specific trades or professions. Since then, industrialization has evolved to the current state of "technologization", the digital transformation taking place in practically every aspect of our lives (head back to Chapter 2 for an exploration of this). Still, we need practical skills and people who have specialized training and hands-on experience in building, maintaining, and repairing our infrastructure and manufacturing goods. These folks provide essential services and play a vital role in the economy. They are well paid for it, and they are always in demand. The Statistics Canada data for 2021 provides the average usual hourly wage by industry based on factors like gender, experience, and location, and utilities workers earn the highest wage, coming in about forty-seven dollars an hour on average.[9] Specialized tradespeople and entrepreneurs command much more.

Here are some quick facts to consider just in my neck of the woods (Ontario):[10]

- One in six job openings are projected to be in the skilled trades by 2026.
- Eighty-five to ninety percent of apprenticeships are paid, on-the-job training.
- Twenty-four thousand six hundred employers offer paid apprenticeships.

---

[9] Statistics Canada (2022): *Quality of Employment in Canada: Average earnings, 1998 to 2021* (www150.statcan.gc.ca).
[10] Please see www.ontario.ca/page/skilled-trades

Electricians, plumbers, carpenters, welders, auto mechanics, machinists, drywallers, bricklayers, equipment operators, painters, medical technicians… they all ensure that our structures function safely and are aesthetically pleasing. They are artists, and the "thinkers" in our world need them to bring their ideas to life.

I once visited High Tech High in San Diego, which was founded by education renaissance man Larry Rosenstock. I campaigned (okay, maybe stalked just a little) to meet Larry for about a year, and finally got the chance at a conference we were both attending. He suggested we escape the event for our meeting and visit the local museum instead.

I liked him immediately. He is one of the most fascinating people I've ever met.

In the back of a cab on a rainy gray day *en route* to a Degas exhibition, he shared that after graduating from Harvard Law School, he decided to become a carpenter, then an educator. The school he founded in 2000 and his innovative approach to education called to me. It just made sense. To this day, High Tech High students work on cross-curricular projects, integrating technology and focusing on real-world application, with a hands-on, experiential learning approach.

What set High Tech High apart was that the "thinkers" worked with the "tinkers" to complete their projects. No streaming involved. Students *built* their learning and made it real. They could point to what they created. An example of a High Tech High student project is "A Fight With Gravity",[11] where kids researched, conducted, and tracked physics experiments about gravity. Then, they built their own kites, balloons, and other objects that could fly.

The culture of the school community at High Tech High is based on

---

[11] High Tech High (2021): *A Fight With Gravity*
(www.hightechhigh.org/project/a_fight_with_gravity).

respect for every child's skills. No skill is favoured over another, and students learn that they need one another to be successful; that they have to collaborate. To this day, everyone at High Tech High contributes — everyone has something to offer — and therefore, everyone is smart and valued. They all fly.

Educators in any type of school system can leverage the High Tech High methodology. Subject areas don't have to be taught in silos, independently, or separately. They can be melded together for a project-based learning, or PBL, approach (see Glossary) that meets many curricular outcomes in one shot and that allows kids with different talents to work together.

Think of how your school day was divided when you were younger. You probably did literacy for a chunk of time, then switched to math, maybe social studies next. Lunch. History. Physical education. Then maybe music or art. And finally, the bell rings for home time! Well, that structure can be wiped away, and students can instead spend the whole day making kites *without* switching subjects and learn all of the subjects in one flow.

Let's look at the learning that teachers can deliver for a kite making unit:

- Science: Students can learn about the principles of aerodynamics, lift, drag, and gravity as they design and build their kites. They can experiment with different shapes, materials, and designs to understand how they affect the flight characteristics of the kite.
- Mathematics: Kite making provides opportunities for students to apply mathematical concepts such as measurement, geometry, and proportions. Students can calculate dimensions for the kite's frame, determine angles for optimal flight, and use geometric shapes in their designs.
- Art and design: Students can explore creativity and artistic expression

as they design and decorate their kites. They can experiment with colors, patterns, and materials to create visually appealing designs, incorporating elements of art and design principles.

- History and culture: Kite making has a rich cultural history and significance in many cultures around the world. Teachers can incorporate facts about the cultural and historical significance of kites. Students can explore the origins, traditions, and cultural practices associated with kite flying.
- Engineering and technology: Kite making involves elements of engineering and technology. Students can design, build, and test their kites, learn about the engineering design process, problem-solve, and innovate as they iterate on their designs to improve performance.
- Physical education: Kite flying provides opportunities for outdoor physical activity and recreation. Students can learn about coordination, balance, and spatial awareness as they maneuver their kites in the air, promoting physical fitness and active play.
- Language arts: Students can engage in writing activities such as journaling or storytelling, or write instructions for kite making. They can also explore existing literature related to kites, such as folktales, poetry, or historical accounts of kite flying adventures.

The purpose of education is to help our youth discover their passions and prepare them for meaningful, contributive careers so that they can become healthy, happy, responsible, active citizens. Young minds *and* young hands need to be nurtured.

Parents' markers of success for themselves often involve having a good job and good health, stability, *and* satisfaction. The trades offer all those things, especially given the shortages we are facing in various skilled and vocational occupations in many countries today (an aging workforce, the societal perception of the trades, and high demand all contribute to this gap). So, parents, take pride in your budding "makers" and "fixers". The trades require craftsmanship, proficiency, and creative problem solving. Revisit your own beliefs, if necessary, and give your child the chance to explore skilled work, if that is what calls to them. Tradespeople have an important role to play in our world, and their talents and the work they do are gifts.

R's creations are unique and customized. He has high standards, and he brings his entire spirit to his craft. Larry Rosenstock would applaud him, and so can we.

Artists

Artists are divergent thinkers. Through the ages, their innovation and creativity has challenged our thinking and beliefs, opening our hearts and minds with messages that shape our culture. They speak a universal language that connects our human experiences.

Creators connect us and move us forward. They are in the business of transformation, and their currency is emotion. A song, painting, story, poem, or dance can have the power to evoke deep, visceral reactions that can unlock the true, fascinating beauty of being alive for us humans. Artists plug into something universal and unconscious and bring it forward, like beacons of light. With passion, sensitivity, curiosity, and perseverance, their creativity is a language that asks us to think about how we are different and how we are the same. They work through and explore pain, beauty, injustice, horror, tragedy, redemption, love, heartbreak... every essence of the human experience. Yet they often travel difficult roads to "make it", and they don't always excel in school. Think Lady Gaga, Eminem, Jennifer Lawrence, Quentin Tarantino, Van Gogh, and

Davinci. We continue to emphasize literacy and numeracy — those three Rs — in our school systems. Art doesn't carry the same weight in them.

In some countries, like Denmark, Norway, New Zealand, Sweden, Canada, and Australia, play-based learning in early education continues until children are up to seven or eight years old, and this approach fosters creativity, social skills, emotional intelligence, and developmental and cognitive growth through free play, outdoor activities, exploration, and experimentation. Brazilian educator and philosopher Paulo Freire based his pedagogy on the concept of "conscientization", focusing on creating awareness and growth with these activities through a lens of social justice for marginalized communities.[12]

Most countries don't have it exactly right yet, though. After you turn eight years old, it's time to stop all that silliness and get down to business!

Pablo Picasso, one of the most influential artists of the twentieth century, was bang on when he said, "Every child is an artist. The problem is how to remain an artist once we grow up."[13] With a big whoosh, however, we erase the innate ways of being that children naturally exhibit and direct them to more "serious" endeavours once they reach a certain (arbitrary) age.

I once had a parent come to me for advice about her son, "P", who wanted to be a writer but refused to share anything he had written with her. She insisted he study functions and relations throughout high school to ensure he could get a "good" job when he graduated, because, "What's he going to do with English?"

There's nothing innately wrong with functions and relations, but P hated it. It was the class he was currently doing worst in (grades wise). So, while I agreed that he needed to achieve the preliminary requirements in

---

[12] Education PD (2022): *Paulo Freire's: Conscientization* (educationpd.com).

[13] Sourced from *Time* Magazine (1976): *Modern Living: Ozmosis in Central Park* (https://content.time.com/time/subscriber/article/0,33009,918412-1,00.html).

mathematics for his high school diploma, I tried to help her understand that even though she worried about his mathematical skills, knowing how to plug the formula for a linear function might not be the best use of his artistic talents. Why torture him? Instead, I suggested she help him explore the many careers in which writing is a necessary skill. If he chose to pursue a career where functions was needed, he could always pick it up when necessary.

Ultimately, she let him know that she loved him no matter what and that his choices were valued. She also agreed that functions just wasn't his thing. With time, trust, and consistency, I hope and want to believe P will be open to sharing his writing with his mother someday.

There are a lot of ways to integrate the arts into current pedagogy and curriculum so that we aren't wiping out something that is joyful to most children. I once taught measurements to a third grade class with a dance and song that the students created themselves after I introduced the lesson. It was fun, and their marks went up in math. There are also teachers who allow students in the higher grades to demonstrate their learning by creating and submitting artwork.

Students should be given choices and opportunities to express themselves, so we can protect them from those strong winds that threaten to extinguish their individual flames. If P had had the opportunity to write a short story about how to solve the equations he was learning about, the math might have been easier for him and he might have found some relevance for functions and relations in his daily life.

Conclusion: They Can't Be Doctors If They Can't Spell

We are at a real inflection point in our evolution right now. Deep, impactful change is essential if we are to shift and transform.

In my corporate days, we had the expression, "We're building the plane as we fly it." Sounds insane to me. Who would jump on *that* ride? Well, educators are in the midst of such a moment, where they are implementing new approaches that are still evolving. They don't have all the answers, and it's important to understand that they are on a plane whose wings aren't fully formed yet. They're still learning, too.

As we collectively and consciously ask ourselves what our values are, what kind of world we live in, and who we truly are in this time of chaos, let's remember the ancient phase from Sun Tzu's *The Art of War*: "With chaos comes opportunity." With this chaos in our educational system comes the opportunity for us to evaluate what has worked for education systems previously and what no longer serves students now.

Alongside the fundamental essential academic aptitudes of reading, writing, and arithmetic, there are technical skills that students can explore so they can find pathways to careers in the trades. Manual dexterity, hand-eye coordination, problem-solving, social skills, adaptability, and creativity are just as important as the ability to produce a scholarly essay. Vocational education is an integral part of our system, and it is crucial to address the skills gap here.

Similarly, budding artists with out-of-the-box ideas are going to lead the way as we move into a very different reality, and our ideas that art isn't as important as some of the other subject areas doesn't support the kids who are born to create. The life of an artist shouldn't be so hard, and if we allow expression and creativity to permeate the workplace, we will all win.

If you observe either of these talents (i.e., aptitude in the trades or the arts) in your young superstars, you might consider having a conversation with their teacher to discuss their skills. We can shift our attitudes and celebrate these kids alongside their "academic" peers, and teachers are in a position to help simply by calling out, acknowledging, and celebrating technical and artistic kids too. Teachers *and* parents can build their awareness of the behaviours and attitudes that are characteristic of big/divergent thinkers and start modeling these attributes themselves. This is the first step to helping kids do the same and find out what works for them.

Teacher Talk Tips

Parents should ask their child's teacher:

- Are you aware of the global learning competencies? How do you integrate them into your teaching practice and assessment?
- What forms of assessment do you use to evaluate my child's learning?
- What is the best way for my child to show you what they know?
- Do you incorporate varied forms of assessment to grade my child?
- Beyond art, are there opportunities for my child to "get their hands dirty"?
- Do you have "maker spaces" in your classroom?
- Do you allow students to show and apply their learning by creating something?
- Are there manipulatives, such as blocks, scales, trays, dice, and measuring tapes, that allow for hands-on exploration of abstract concepts in your classroom?
- Do you provide examples of real-world applications for learning?
- Do you assess practical tasks, projects, and theoretical understanding of concepts?
- Do you showcase artwork and student creations by putting them on display?

Parents should think about:

- Whether their child defines themselves according to how well they score.
- What messages they give their child regarding their scores.
- How they react to a "bad" mark.
- What behaviours they are modelling to their child.
- Whether their child shows signs of advanced gross and fine motor skills.
- Whether their child exhibits physical abilities and coordination, like hand-eye coordination, spatial awareness, or a high degree of competence using tools like scissors, gadgets, or even musical instruments.
- Whether their child excels in sports.
- Whether their child has high levels of creativity, imagination, and observational skills.
- Whether their child is gifted in expressive communication, drawing, painting and problem-solving.

Consider also your child's needs:
- What is their attitude toward their marks?
- Do they suffer from test anxiety? Do they need emotional support?
- Are there any barriers to their learning? Do they need extra support or accommodation?
- Do they need support with time management and organizational skills?
- Have you asked them what they think they need to be successful? Have you asked them what success looks like to them?
- Do they strongly integrate information when they can see, touch, and manipulate objects?
- Would they benefit from an apprenticeship or internship?
- Are there opportunities for you to expose them to careers in the trades?

- Are there opportunities for them to participate in artistic activities outside school, such as art camps or art events?

As a teacher, the biggest gift I can receive is when I get to watch a student grow and develop. It's an honour to see the workings of a child's mind when they are truly engaged, determined, and delighted to integrate new learning into their lives. Those moments are special and can never, ever be defined by a mark. Two plus two is four, yes, but understanding how and why a student gets to four, and then watching them apply that knowledge (whether they draw it, sing about it, or build blocks to express the concept), is what we can applaud and celebrate. Focus on the learning and growth, not the score. In this new world, we can support children to show up in all their glory; in full expression of who they are.

S was unstoppable in the third grade, even though she couldn't spell. Maybe she was a fixer or an artist. Either way, I hope she got a shot to shine, just like Lulu did.

4

NEURODIVERSITY AND SPECIAL EDUCATION: OUT-OF-THE-BRAIN THINKING, DOING, AND BEING

Neurodiversity

MY FIRST EXPERIENCE WITH NEURODIVERSITY was almost twenty years ago, when I was working with Janis Lundman and Adrienne Mitchell of Back Alley Films, Canada. Janis and Adrienne are strong, creative, and successful women in the Canadian film industry. They had hired me on the spot after a discussion about my skills and choice of nail polish colour (it was fluorescent green, and it sealed the deal). They shared that they were interested in developing a female character on the autism spectrum in one of their upcoming projects, a doctor that worked with the police to solve crimes. It was my task to learn everything about autism and help create the character.

Away I went.

Janis and Adrienne were ahead of their time. Sadly, there was no appetite for the show. However, what I learned during that time was critical for me and my foray into education some years later. Armed with this experience and a boatload of empathy, my approach to working with neurodiverse students became my teaching practice for *all* students. However, it was "V", a ten-year-old who seemed to float through school, who really showed me the way.

I was the go-to supply teacher for a multiple exceptionalities class for a year, and the experience and life lessons I garnered from my time with V and six other students continue to colour my view of the world. These kids had a combination of what was described as "learning disorders", "impairments", or physical disabilities, and required additional support and "special" education (but let's note that this is "deficit" language, and it's preferable to focus on what kids *can* do, not what they can't). I looked for ways to give these kids opportunities to join in the regular classroom environment and integrate them for short periods of time where possible. We all worked hard to teach these kids how to fit into and function in our world so they could succeed in society and lead what we considered to be fulfilling lives.

During one lesson with the lovely V, the lights went on for me: I had it backwards. I had been tasked with teaching her about texture—the difference between "rough" and "smooth"—and I'd kept repeating the words and showing her pictures with examples of each (like a cotton ball versus sandpaper). Whenever I showed her a new set of pictures, she just smiled her ethereal smile, looking at me but not *looking* at me.

I quickly realized I was getting nowhere fast.

I can't say what prompted my epiphany, but I took her hand and ran it through the dimply beige brick wall we were sitting by, and then did the same thing with the floor we were sitting on. I said nothing; I just kept repeating this motion. I only paired the words with the wall when I thought V was ready to hear them. First, I had to get into her world, and suddenly, I understood how to.

In one incredible, joyful moment for us both, we truly connected, and she was able to take various objects and tell me their textures by the end of the class.

The prevalence of autism spectrum disorders has been steadily increasing over the past few decades. Whether this is due to increased awareness, changes in diagnostic criteria, earlier detection, or even environmental factors, we don't know. Irrespective, neurodivergence now covers a range of highly complex neurodevelopmental disorders that can differ from person to person, with symptoms ranging from mild to severe. People on the spectrum can exhibit differences in social communication and interaction, can have restricted or repetitive behaviours, and can experience sensory sensitivities. Neurodiversity is very personal.

I think it's magic.

The Māori are an Indigenous Polynesian people of New Zealand that have a rich cultural heritage, including distinctive language, traditions, arts, and customs. In 2017, Keri Opai, the Māori strategic lead for the Te Pou Nui organization, coined the te reo Māori (the Māori language) term for autism: *takiwātanga*. This means "in my/his/her own time and space".

I am not a doctor or a medical health professional. However, I think it's safe to say our research hasn't gone far enough for us to understand what's going on with the circuitry of neurodiverse brains (and I will include ADHD in this category, which is also currently defined as a brain-based disorder that manifests in symptoms of inattention, hyperactivity, and impulsivity). Neurodiversity can be so varied from person to person because different neural pathways can be affected—some jammed, some blocked, and some inactive.

We refer to neurodiversity as a "dis"-order, which is, by definition, a disturbance in "normal" functioning, structures, or behaviours. This means we see the neurodiverse as impaired in some way. But what if, like the Māori, we changed these attitudes and gave our beliefs an upgrade? Young children don't differentiate, judge, or define what's "normal". In their purest moments, they accept one another and adapt to each other's needs. Similarly, if we slow down for a second, sit, and accept and appreciate how the neurodiverse "are" on this planet, we can see that they can show us a very different perspective to life on earth. We should give the neurodiverse space to exist alongside everyone else, without them being expected to mask, hide, or camouflage their true nature in order to adopt what we perceive as more "typical" and "socially acceptable" behaviours. There's no need for them to supress their unique selves. Besides, it's exhausting for them to constantly bury their natural behaviours to fit in. In fact, this has detrimental effects on their overall health.

I recall attending a ceremony where eighth grade students were being awarded a certificate, and at one point in the procession, a young man who was on the spectrum approached the teacher with joy, glee, and excitement to accept his document. The audience laughed along with him. The women sitting near me, who I knew to be kind, stated, "Poor thing."

I gently leaned over and said, "There's nothing poor about him. He's so happy, experiencing this moment in his own way, and he's invited us to share his joy. Isn't that a gift to us?"

Neurotypical behaviour isn't the "default", and we should embrace this uniqueness. Let the neurodiverse stim, avoid eye contact, and express themselves when they become overstimulated (including having meltdowns). We can accept neurodiversity in all its glory so that it becomes as natural to us as walking past someone who has a different hair colour than we do.

This young man from this example, V, and others like them are what I call "heartworkers". My own moment of understanding with V helped me to see that while I had been so busy imposing my way of being onto her, I had been learning about and reminded of the following traits from her:

- Patience.
- Kindness.
- Presence.
- Delight.
- Openness.
- Gentleness.
- Stillness.
- Simplicity.
- Compassion.
- Generosity.

In short, I believe that as we were working together, V wasn't looking through me at all; she was looking right at me, mirroring and magnifying all the aspects of myself I could work on.

There are already programs out there which socialize and teach neurodiverse students skills so they can function in the neurotypical world. This isn't the book where you'll find that information, so please seek that elsewhere and get your child all the help they need. Alongside this support, however, we can take a deep breath and consider the qualities listed previously as some of the competencies required for a new world that we can build together. These competencies need to be modelled and affirmed to all students. Don't you agree?

I always encourage parents of a neurotypical (not neurodivergent) children who do well in the current school game to encourage their child to help another student who may be struggling more than them, even if that means their child will have to slow down their quest to get to and stay at the top of the mountain. I tell these parents that the mountain isn't going anywhere. Yes, it is true that we reward the quickest students — the ones who can climb effortlessly — but we know that in life, it's ultimately not about getting to the top quickly and staking a claim. The learning is in the climbing, and there are many different ways to climb. Besides, as the saying goes, it can be very lonely at the top.

This is not always a popular approach, but many systems are integrating all students in one classroom environment. Teachers can't "teach to the middle"; they must create programming that is responsive to all, and this takes more time and effort. The payoff can be really sweet, though. My workaround for this was to create every lesson as if I was teaching a supported (formerly known as special) education class (we'll talk about those next). If used wisely, machines (e.g., AI) can also help to free up a teacher's time, so that their focus can stay on helping students learn human skills, beyond the subjects they are hired to teach (you'll read more about that in the next chapter).

We also can't forget "gifted" students. They also have different views of the world and may also happen to be neurodivergent. They need opportunities to extend and explore their learning, while others work at a slower pace and most land somewhere in the middle. The key is to radically remove our judgements about how each child operates. The gifted child is no more deserving of praise than the child who needs varied approaches to learning. It's not a race. Even if it was, let's not forget who wins in Aesop's *The Tortoise and the Hare*.

We can't oversimplify or discount the difficult moments parents of children with different needs tackle day in and day out, but we can acknowledge that each child is having their own subjective experience. Parents can give their children space to learn at their own pace, and teachers can work to bring to light the different talents and abilities of every student.

That's big love.

"Special" Education and Students with "Disabilities"

"Special education" refers to educational programs and support services designed to meet the unique needs of students with disabilities or special needs. Such students often have learning disabilities, intellectual disabilities, physical disabilities, developmental delays, behavioural disorders, sensory impairments, and other health impairments. The goal of special education is to provide these students with the necessary accommodations, modifications, and individualized instruction to help them succeed academically, socially, and emotionally.

Key aspects of special education include:

- Individualized education plans (IEPs). Students with disabilities are typically provided with an IEP, which is a personalized plan outlining their specific learning goals, instructional strategies, support services, and accommodations. The IEP is developed collaboratively by educators, parents or guardians, and other relevant professionals, and it is regularly reviewed and updated to ensure the student's needs are being met.

- Differentiated instruction. Special education teachers and support staff employ various instructional strategies and techniques to meet the diverse needs of students with disabilities. These may include adapting the curriculum, using multisensory approaches, providing visual aids, offering additional support or reinforcement, and utilizing assistive technologies.

- Related services. In addition to academic instruction, students with disabilities may receive related services to address their individual needs. These services can include speech therapy, occupational therapy, physical therapy, counseling, social skills training, and behaviour intervention.

- Inclusive practices. Special education aims to promote the inclusion and participation of students with disabilities in the general education environment to the maximum extent possible. Inclusive practices involve providing appropriate supports and accommodations (to ensure that students with disabilities have equal access to educational opportunities and are integrated into classroom activities and social interactions with their peers).

- Collaboration and support. Special education often involves collaboration among educators, specialists, parents or guardians, and other stakeholders, to ensure that students receive comprehensive support and services. This collaboration may include regular communication, team meetings, professional development, and coordination of resources.

- Transition planning. For students with disabilities who are transitioning to adulthood, special education may include transition planning, to help them prepare for postsecondary education, vocational training, employment, or independent living. Transition planning focuses on developing skills, exploring career options, and accessing community resources to support successful transitions.

Overall, special education plays a crucial role in ensuring that students with disabilities receive the support and resources they need to reach their full potential and achieve success in school and beyond. It is guided by the principles of equity, inclusion, and individualized support to address the diverse needs of students with disabilities.

But just a second. Throughout this section, I've used the current "deficit" nomenclature we often use to describe students who require individualized supports and accommodations in the classroom so that they can learn in their own ways. But this just doesn't sit right with me. V and others like her, including all kids with what we call "disabilities" or those who require support that we label "special education", challenge our ideas about what it means to live fully.

Why is this "special"? Aren't all kids special? In my mind, it's "supported education" we're describing here, not "special education". Furthermore, "disabled" kids aren't "dis"-abled at all; they are *differently* abled. Therefore, I choose to use the word "diffability" instead of "disability". These unique expressions of our abilities are among the most beautiful aspects of life.

I'd like to push us to change our attitudes, starting with the language we are currently using toward the "disabled". What happens if we replace "special" with "supported" and "disabilities" with "diffabilites" in the section you just read? Check out Appendix E.

Why Do Kids Become Targets for Bullying?

The "diffabled", like any child who is perceived as weaker or vulnerable, often have a hard time making friends and can become victims of bullying. This is a serious issue that can have harmful, lifelong effects on kids. Bullying is repeated, aggressive behaviour intended to intimidate, harm, or exert power over another, and it takes physical form (e.g., hitting and kicking), verbal form (e.g., name calling and teasing), social form (e.g., spreading rumors and excluding someone from social activities), or cyberbullying form (e.g., harassment, threats, and spreading rumors online).

When bullying is in the picture, our children's health and safety is compromised—or, worse, at risk. It can have significant negative effects on the target's physical and emotional wellbeing, leading to issues such as low self-esteem, depression, anxiety, academic difficulties, and, in severe cases, self-harm or suicide.

Bullying often involves repeated incidents or a pattern of behaviour over time rather than isolated incidents. There is typically a power imbalance between the bully and the target, with the bully exerting control or dominance over the target. This behaviour is usually intentional and aimed at causing harm, distress, or fear.

Our friends at UNESCO released a report in 2019 (updated in 2023) that presented data from one hundred and forty-four countries.[14] Much to my dismay, it confirmed that school violence and bullying are major worldwide problems. The report states:

> *Almost one in three students (32%) have been bullied by their peers at school "at least once in the last month", and a similar proportion are affected by physical violence. Physical bullying is the most frequent type of bullying in many regions, with the exception of North America and Europe, where psychological bullying is most common. Sexual bullying is the second most common in many regions. School violence and bullying affects both male and female students. Physical bullying is more common among boys, while psychological bullying is more prevalent among girls. Online and mobile phone bullying is also shown to be increasing. The second most frequent reasons reported by students relate to race, nationality or colour.*

Isn't this just terrible? There is absolutely no question about it: we must protect children who are bullied. Yet we also have to examine and change the behaviour of the bully, to prevent them from going on to find another victim. Think about it: if a child thinks they have to hurt someone who they think is weak to feel powerful and better about themselves, they are the ones who are indeed powerless and weak. Who is bullying them? The

---

[14] UNESCO (2019): *School violence and bullying a major global issue, new UNESCO publication finds* (www.unesco.org/en/articles/school-violence-and-bullying-major-global-issue-new-unesco-publication-finds).

bully is the one who inflicts harm, but they are also a child in pain themselves.

There's no single, simple answer to why kids become bullies. However, we can call out a few indicators that can lead a child to behave so poorly.

We know bullying is a power play for kids who suffer from low self-esteem. Bullying is, essentially, attention seeking behaviour (even if the attention is negative) to gain control or perhaps social status. Bullies can also learn to be aggressive from others in their circle, like their own parents, peers, and what they see in the media. Sadly, an unhealthy family environment where there is inconsistent or harsh discipline, exposure to violence, or lack of supervision can lead these kids to model what's going on at home, in school. Sometimes, a child may even have difficulty understanding or empathizing with the feelings of others. They may lack the emotional intelligence or social skills necessary to understand and manoeuvre social interactions positively. Bullying behaviour may also be a manifestation of other underlying issues, like academic difficulties, mental health issues, or experiences of trauma or abuse.

At the end of the day, these kids are looking for a way to cope with their stress and frustration. They are fruitlessly looking for ways to feel better about themselves. They need help to understand the causes of their behaviour and to correct it.

Prevention and intervention strategies are a must. We cannot excuse or accept bullying under any circumstances. Prevention efforts should focus on promoting empathy, respect, and positive relationships, as well as providing support and resources.

But what about the child who is affected by the torment? Why did that child get chosen, and how do we help them?

No child ever deserves to be bullied. We know the "diffabled", the vulnerable, the socially isolated "outsiders" (i.e., the "loners"), and those that are different in some way (like kids who identify as LGBTQ+) get picked on because they often can't defend themselves. We can even include kids who are different in appearance or academic ability here: kids who are "quirky", or are overweight or underweight, or have braces or glasses, or get lower grades or higher grades, can also be harassed and tormented.

The bullied must be taught to tell a trusted adult if they are being mistreated in any way. These people can help the bullied learn strategies to stand up for themselves assertively by setting clear, firm, and consistent boundaries. All children have the right to feel safe and supported in their schools and communities, and it's essential to address bullying behaviour and promote positive social dynamics to prevent harm and create inclusive environments for all children. It's a parent's natural, innate instinct to protect their children, and they should do so at all costs, no questions asked.

There's no doubt that the bullied needs our attention and care; their pain and suffering is obvious. Not so much with the bully; their pain is hidden under layers of agony, struggle, and conflict. When we're addressing bullying, we need to question what we value and what it means to achieve harmony in the way we treat one another (and how we do it). Here's a suggestion for a revolutionary act: be kind to a bully, if you can. Maybe this can help to turn them around.

We need to rethink our priorities. When inspirational teachers and parents acknowledge, practice, and reward a certain behaviour, it is normalized, and students follow suit.

Conclusion: Neurodiversity and Special Education

Teachers are hired to deliver a curriculum that is approved and assigned by their local Ministries or Departments of Education. It's their job to do so. It's mandated. They also hold space for something very precious: your child's spirit.

We have to believe that they care deeply about their students. Let's remember that they are human, they burn out, and they, too, are learning. Recognize vulnerability, passion, commitment, and exhaustion, and see them as people. Be the person you want them to be with your child. It can start with you.

Teacher Talk Tips

Parents should ask their child's teacher:
- What is your favourite thing about my child? How is that respected, celebrated, and acknowledged in your classroom? How are these attitudes modelled?
- How do you allow my child to express themselves in varied ways in your teaching practice?
- What strategies do you use to redirect my child if they are struggling?
- Can I share what we do at home to keep consistency in both environments?
- Can we schedule regular discussions so we can reflect, revise, and align our approach and make it uniform?
- How do you handle bullying or peer conflicts in the classroom, and what support is available for students who are affected by this?
- How do you normalize behaviour that may be viewed as odd?
- How do you model kindness and inclusion in your classroom?
- How will you protect and nurture my child's spirit?

Parents should think about:
- What their favourite thing about their child is.

- How they show up for and connect with their child.
- Whether they can regulate themselves first, before they attempt to regulate their child.
- What their child needs from them when the child is triggered, and how they will learn and practice this behaviour (reread the list of qualities V taught me from earlier in this chapter and add your own points).
- What their child is teaching *them*.
- What else can be a positive influence on their child.

Consider also your child's needs:
- When are they most happy? Calm? Engaged?
- What are the moments when you find yourself most happy, calm, and engaged with them? (Are these the same as your answer to the previous question?)
- What are their needs?
- Do they enjoy their learning environment? Are their needs being met in it?
- How do they need to be loved?
- How do they communicate? Cognitively? Physically? Emotionally?

Neurodiverse and differently abled people can be highly sensitive, and sadly, they are often punished for it. They are not to be feared, ridiculed, or mistreated because they can be more "tapped in" and can connect to something deeper that exists within all of us. V and others like her are here to live their lives on their own terms, and they can help us to embody the parts of our innate nature that are kind and inclusive. Their actions and creations are a call to us to examine, change by learning how to "be", and use our talents right now, in this moment in history, because we need left-of-center, creative solutions to help us evolve.

Celebrate the achievements your child makes in their own time, in their own way. Pay attention to what they are showing you about yourself and reset accordingly, if need be. Learn their language and then accept and savour their gifts with curiosity, wonder, and love. Let's allow the grace in ourselves to make room for those who are different; to lead us to start thinking and doing with our hearts. They are the ones who shine brilliantly. They are asking us to see them, and they are teaching us how to lead enriching lives.

5

NEW TEACHER: RETHINKING OUR VALUES AND HOW WE DO SCHOOL (PART 1)

———

I WAS ONCE INVITED TO speak at a local college for the kickoff of their new twenty-first century strategy to transform education.[15] They asked me to envision (and share my vision of) a job in education that didn't yet exist. You can bet I was all in, because I got to reimagine school — particularly the role of the teacher.

Remember the all-knowing holder of information, "sage on the stage" teaching style from Chapter 1? Some big thinkers and researchers have helped identify approaches to help us evolve from that. These are as follows.

1. Guide on the Side/Facilitator (Alice Johnson)

"The teacher for the gifted and talented will be more of [a] 'guide on the

———

[15] Please see www.georgebrown.ca/sites/default/files/workshift-podcast-episode-6-transcript.pdf

side' rather than a 'sage on the stage'." This seems to have first been said in 1981 by Alice Johnson, a secondary teacher in Kentucky, USA.[16]

The "guide on the side" approach contrasts with and moves on from the "sage on the stage" approach. In the former, the teacher no longer acts as the central figure that imparts all the information to passive students who are to listen attentively, gobble up every word, and then spit it back out to be graded. Instead, teachers act as facilitators and supporters who practice student centered instruction to activate learning. They do this by asking a lot of questions to provide guidance and resources. They kickstart thinking and discussion. Most importantly, they set up opportunities for kids to explore concepts, solve problems, and construct their own meanings from the material they are studying. This approach is inquiry-based and active. It fosters student engagement and independence.

2. Synthesizer/Activator (John Hattie)[17]

The "synthesizer/activator" role is also a more modern teaching approach, but steps it up one more notch. In this approach, educators continue to stimulate those twenty-first century global competencies (as they are usually encouraged to do in the modern classroom environment), including curiosity, critical thinking, and communication, to activate learning. Then, they add a layer on top: to synthesize learning, "synthesizer/activator" teachers engage students to integrate the information they have already acquired with what they are learning, to

---

[16]*Harlan Daily Enterprise* (1981): *'Gifted Students' Classes Offered.* Sourced from a Google News Archive search (news.google.com/newspapers).

[17] Hattie, J. (2008): *Visible Learning: A Synthesis of Over 800 Meta-Analyses Relating to Achievement* (minerva-access.unimelb.edu.au/bitstream).

make connections and create something new. They are constantly evaluating their teaching approaches, reflecting critically on students' needs, and creating dynamic classroom environments to strategically nudge students toward optimal learning outcomes.

This sounds like fun for both teachers and students. It allows for reciprocity. Teachers need to be adaptable and to stay on their toes, creating engaging learning experiences for children, and they can learn how to do so from their students (if they approach with an open heart), just like V did with me. The "synthesizer/activator" approach fosters connection and creativity.

"Connection" and "creativity", as hallmarks of student success, should ring a bell. They are on the list of global competencies teachers need to prioritize.

Let's build on all this goodness and find our footing on a possible new rung: we'll follow connection and creativity with a good dash of curiosity (which leads to purpose), so that students can contribute to the world in their chosen career with passion. If I could make this a math equation, it might look like this:

$$\text{Connection} + \text{Creativity (Curiosity)} *$$
$$(\text{Purpose} * \text{Contribution}) = \text{PASSION}$$

Now all we need is dedicated, multifaceted individuals with experience in teaching, psychology, data analytics, and guidance, to execute. This leads us to...

3. Career Calling Coach (Lia De Cicco Remu)

Trained, accredited professionals and educators can act as child psychology practitioners, child health specialists, and data scientists. These are Career Calling Coaches, or CCCs. They are synthesizers who capture students' growth as soon as they enter our education system and who keep track of evidence of learning, to help create a roadmap that will support the student in finding their calling and embarking upon a satisfying career. You can think of CCCs as synthesizers who are keenly aware of every student's spirit and who understand when to gently, respectfully challenge students with the question, "What do you want to you do about this problem you're facing right now in your learning? Where do you want to go with it? How?"

In Ontario, students must enrol in a half-year careers studies course when they are in high school. Here, they start to think about what they want to do after graduation. They are fourteen and fifteen years of age when they meet a career studies teacher who is tasked with the job of helping them to navigate the rest of their lives, in a few short months. I am pleased to be collaborating with one of the largest school boards in Canada that is piloting a transformative careers curriculum resources for the tenth grade and is considering the same for kindergarten, fourth grade, and eighth grade (during the transition to ninth grade).

This is great work. I hope there is groupthink going on out there and that others are also building out this approach.

Ultimately, the goal is to have CCCs guide and activate students in every grade on their paths, and then identify their passions before transmuting them into action.

Let's have some fun and add to our word math to see what we get:

$$\text{Connection} + \text{Creativity (Curiosity)} * (\text{Purpose} * \text{Calling} + \text{Contribution}) = \text{HAPPINESS} + \text{PASSION (ACTION)}$$

Isn't the development of happy, fulfilled adults who bring their greatest gifts to society the endgame of school?

More fun:

$$Connection + Creativity (Curiosity) * (Purpose * Calling + Contribution) = HAPPINESS$$

$$PASSION + ACTION = GOALS$$

If our imagined CCCs successfully support this new paradigm of human student growth, our students can develop a clearer idea about their goals. Think about how many kids you know who have clarity about this, and how many (on the other hand) moan when asked, "What do you want to be when you grow up?".

Younger kids can tell you all kinds of interesting things. Among my favourite responses from five-year-olds are:

- "I want to feed monkeys."
- "I want to be a professional hugger."
- "I want to paint all the trucks red."

So cute! But what happens after the third grade, when we focus on "schooling" them and, sadly, they forget who they are?

To examine this, let's dig into those responses given by the five-year-olds. They hold precious clues about how kids might like to bring themselves into the world:

- Feeding monkeys can be parlayed into all kinds of careers centered on working with animals. Perhaps, alternatively, this child will be a chef.
- Professional huggers actually exist nowadays (they're called cuddlers), but there might alternatively be a budding teacher, psychologist, social worker, doctor, or some form of caregiver here.
- Painting trucks red? An artist, or maybe a skilled tradesperson.

This innocence speaks volumes about their personalities and inclinations, and such answers must be gathered, stored, reviewed, and revised to match the fluidity that students experience when they are children. This data must move with them as they mature.

Currently, in my home province of Ontario, an Ontario student record is a legislated, mandated document that holds each student's identification and educational progress (like report cards, transcripts, or information that might help improve instruction for them). At the beginning of every school year, teachers receive their new students' files. Yet this information could be much more fulsome, and could be a more formalized space for identifying student passion. The CCC approach calls on teachers to take this data and integrate it into their lessons, to motivate and excite students about their learning.

Let's say a bright-eyed five-year-old comes to kindergarten with a fascination for tigers. Their kindergarten teacher picks up on this and includes it in their student record accordingly, along with some sample work that is aligned with curricular outcomes. Here's how the journey might go as more data about the child is collected and compiled:

1. Kindergarten: Draws a tiger.
2. First grade: Draws a tiger and writes the word "tiger".
3. Second grade: Writes a sentence about tigers.
4. Third grade: Writes a paragraph about tigers and indicates interest in tiger habitats.
5. Fourth to sixth grade: Investigates how the environment affects tiger habitats. Writes about this using math like data management, probability, patterning, number sense, and measurement, to express findings regarding the impact of climate change.
6. Seventh to eighth grade: Finds other students who are passionate about climate change and its effects on animal life. Works on a collaborative project designed to inform others with peers.

7. Ninth to twelfth grade: Sources industries working on climate change and begins to build their network. Expands on the projects they worked on from fourth to eighth grade, perhaps reaching out to students around the world to broaden their network and create a community. Creates a not-for-profit.

Note that this is very tidy and linear, and most students won't have such a clear-cut path. Still, let's focus on what teachers can do to champion and support the unfolding of students' spirits. This will always be so much more meaningful than grading thirty paragraphs for grammar on "what I did on my summer holidays". The machines can do that!

Technology and the Career Calling Coach (CCC) Model

First off, we need to reframe the tiger journey above, because technology allows students to jump around and find themselves in it at different points. Joanne McEachen pointed this out to me, and she's right. Instead, with the use of technology, it could go more like this:

1. Kindergarten: Searches for pictures of tigers on the Internet. Draws a tiger and writes the word "tiger".
2. First to third grade: Collects tiger songs and videos and learns that tigers can live in different habitats across Asia, like rainforests, grasslands, mountains, and even swamps.
3. Fourth to sixth grade: Finds tiger habitat sites and connects with other kids who are also passionate about animal life. Works on a collaborative project designed to inform others with peers. Sources industries that are working on climate change and begins to build their network.
4. Seventh to eighth grade: Works and collaborates on a local campaign

to raise awareness of climate change and activates other students to get involved.

5. Ninth to twelfth grade: Creates a not-for-profit. Learns about social marketing and PR and seeks out speaking engagements in partnership with organizations working on climate change. Uses AI to help create marketing content such as videos, press releases and social media posts.

All because of a love for tigers!

Teacher awareness, support, and guidance at key points in this journey are crucial, so they can remove obstacles and keep students moving (like when the student is organizing the local campaign or connecting with organizations outside school). This journey can go in many different directions for a student, and teachers are in a position to provide rocket fuel, helping to launch students into their careers so that "What do you want to be when you grow up?" might become less confusing and agonizing for some students.

All of this information about students' interests and journeys can be housed in cloud-based digital learning portfolios that follow the student, like their OSR (Ontario student record). Every year, teachers upload the student's output. Alternatively (or in addition), beginning in the junior years, this student might create their own "all about me" website, culminating in an end product of learning or a summative that showcases their journey, who they are, and what they have done.

I wonder how many educators reading this are thinking, *Seriously? Don't I have enough on my plate?* Rest assured that there are technological tools that can take care of any overflow, so educators *can* pivot and bring their attention, energy, and heart to their students' human wellbeing and help them figure out who they are becoming. Like I mentioned before, the machines can grade the grammar. Teachers should still check it over, but they should focus more on the process of learning and what the students are revealing about themselves and provide thoughtful, targeted interventions accordingly.

Other than automatic grading and feedback, technology (in particular, AI) can save valuable teacher time. Here are a few such technologies out there right now:

- Data analytics. AI can analyze student data and learning patterns to help teachers identify and build learning paths tailored to individual student needs and uncover strengths, weaknesses, or interests so that learning can be personalized for each child.
- Learning management systems (LMS). These are centralized online spaces where educators can create and organize course materials, administer assessments, facilitate communication with students, and track learners' progress.
- Chatbots and virtual assistants. These tools can provide instant support, answer questions, give study tips, and help with administrative tasks.
- Virtual tutors. AI driven tutors can provide personalized instruction, feedback, and guidance, assisting students with concepts and problem solving.
- Content creation. AI tools can generate lesson plans, quizzes, learning materials, exercises, resources, textbooks, and multimedia presentations. See Appendix F for a sample lesson plan created by ChatGPT on "Exploring Tigers" that took me fifteen seconds to generate. (Remember that AI has a tendency to "hallucinate" and can be biased, so teachers must vet any information that is AI-generated.)
- Virtual and augmented reality. This technology creates immersive learning experiences that let students experience virtual worlds in 3D. We can put our sample student in a simulated tiger habitat!

The queue at Miss B's desk (from Chapter 2) could have been a lot shorter, freeing up her time and increasing student engagement, self-learning, exploration, independence, and creativity, if she had had the opportunity to fuse her pedagogy with technology. She could have been spending her time enjoying getting to know her students.

Kids are already using tech on their own outside school. We now have the ability to ensure this behaviour is directed appropriately for their learning and growth inside our classrooms, too.

Conclusion: New Teacher

Not all teachers are highflyers—the fearless innovators who are comfortable with taking risks, trying different ideas or methods, and catalyzing change in our classrooms—and that's okay. There are often a few in every school who introduce new approaches and influence others to follow suit, but ultimately, it takes time for a full cohort of teachers to learn and adopt new technologies, and this process can be overwhelming.

As teachers become aware of and begin to understand how today's technology can transform their teaching practices, parents can have conversations with their children's teachers to understand how they encourage, validate, and applaud all students. Are they paying attention to who your child is?

Teacher Talk Tips

Parents should ask their child's teacher:
- When my child isn't "paying attention", what do you notice is distracting them from your lesson?

- Do you have check-ins or one-on-one conversations with my child that allow them to explore their likes/dislikes?
- Would you consider doing a "show and tell" activity for clues into student interests that might be developed into passions, and then careers?
- Are you familiar with technologies that can support you with your administrative duties so that you can focus on the human aspect of teaching?
- Do you use data to inform your teaching practice?

Parents should think about:

- When their child is the most joyful, whether they can pull topics, ideas, or interests out of these joyful moments, and whether they are truly present with their child to capture these moments.
- How they can encourage the exploration of the things or activities that excite their child.

Consider also your child's needs:

- Do they have opportunities to muse? Are they overscheduled?
- How do they communicate with you? Are you listening?
- How do you spend time with them? Is it always structured and hurried?

Teaching can be incredibly fulfilling work. It is also very powerful work. Teachers hold much of the space where kids explore the many versions of themselves. They open doors, show roads, and help shape your child's decisions about which paths they wish to take. It takes a lot of energy and focus to catch the moments when a child reveals a passion or an interest, take that information, investigate it further, build on it to create pathways, and allow them to make discoveries about themselves.

Teaching no longer needs to be transactional. It can be deeply rewarding. It's a great gift to witness a child's trajectory and contribute to their growth. That is the true calling of a teacher.

6

PARENTS AS PARTNERS IN EDUCATION: RETHINKING OUR VALUES AND HOW WE DO SCHOOL (PART 2)

The Power of the Parent

THERE'S AN INSPIRATIONAL STORY ABOUT Thomas Edison's mother that has been popularized:

When little Thomas' teacher sent a note home that stated he was "addled" and wouldn't be allowed to attend regular school anymore, Ms. Edison read the letter to Thomas out loud. However, she took some creative license in the retelling. She explained to her son that he was, in fact, a genius, and that school was too slow for *him*. From that point on, the heroic Ms. Edison homeschooled Thomas, and I think we all know what became of him after that.

I believe our thoughts are *things*.[18] They have energy, and they direct our paths. Edison believed his mother when she told him he was a genius,

---

[18] Mulford, P. (1908): *Thoughts Are Things*. Republished in 2007 by Barnes & Noble.

and acted accordingly. If he'd gone with his teacher's summation, maybe we wouldn't have electricity today.

We must be hyperaware of the influence adults have on children. If we tell them they are capable, they will be. Parents are the first line of defence and must be excellent stickhandlers for their children as they learn to navigate life on their own. Parents are busy, but the expectation that they can drop off our kids at school and leave everything to teachers for eight hours is faulty. It's important to acknowledge that a new age that some are calling "The Great Awakening" (not to be confused with the religious revival in eighteenth century colonial America) is occurring, and it represents a new era of enlightenment, transformation, and global harmony. Kids need their parents during this time. Somewhere in all of this, we have to stop hurrying through the world, be gentle with ourselves, and remember that our kids are priority number one.

Teachers are tremendous role models for children, yet in my part of the world, they often get a bad rap. It's sometimes easy to believe that they aren't doing enough to get your child to where you think they should be. A lot of parents today push back or even fight over this, and sometimes, they need to.

There is always a group of parents (mothers, mostly) that is rather active in school life. They participate in parent-teacher councils, run events, attend school trips, and fundraise. They show up - a lot. But let's be realistic: not everyone can, or wants, to have this level of involvement. Still, if you choose to have a high degree of participation, you can develop a meaningful joint decision-making partnership with your child's teacher beyond the timeslot allotted to you for parent-teacher interviews.

Teachers can have up to thirty-five students in their class, and that's a lot to manage if they don't all have access to the tools mentioned in the previous chapter. Still, you, as the parent, have every right to check in and communicate with teachers whenever you feel the need to. Work with them to ask about, understand, and know what they are teaching. Ask for their teaching unit plans for the school year. Research what the curriculum expectations and outcomes are for your child's grade. Then, talk about those topics at home with your child. Create opportunities to supplement and support the material they are learning.

It's possible to integrate school into home life. Your little genius is learning the difference between a city and a town? Go for a drive. Get them to talk to you about what they *learn* in school rather than what they *do* there, and concretize the lessons they're having in class with a real-world experience. Here are some examples of the things you can ask that might help start your journey of connecting their activities to their learning:

- ✓ "What was fun today?" (Helps to gain insight into what interests them.)
- ✓ "What did you do at recess?" (Helps to gauge socio-emotional wellbeing.)
- ✓ "Did your teacher say anything funny today?" (Gets your kids to talk about what they are learning in the context of humour.) If the answer is "no", ask, "Why was it boring?"

Get creative, have fun, and know that you are not alone.

Some parents out there have created resources and assistance that can help with this. I came across one such body in Canada called Let's Get Together, a nonprofit organization founded by Alison Canning that aims to make learning equitable and education accessible.[19] I was once invited to speak to parents about how they can help their kids land good jobs by Let's Get Together, which was an amazing honour.

It's important to acknowledge that there's often a certain level of privilege that goes with understanding how to get access to resources. However, many organizations help *all* parents, regardless of

---

[19] Please see www.letsgettogether.ca

socioeconomic status. Parents Engaged in Education, founded by Theresa Pastore (also in Canada), is one example.[20] I was once lucky enough to meet her on a visit to the family service center and education bank she built, a space that encourages parent engagement and supports low-income families with materials and gives them access to technology.

Alison and Theresa are special souls. With their teams, they do amazing work to help improve parent involvement in their children's academic progress. And groups like these are growing: parents are sitting at tables where education system decisions are made. This is amazing: parents should be heard and can contribute ideas for how school can evolve and be better for every single child, without exception.

What Can School Be?

I've had the chance to work with and think alongside some really smart people, collaborating to make school relevant, engaging, and equitable for all students. Two such people are "M" and "J", who have young children that are about to enter the school system, and who both have experience and knowledge about pedagogy, curriculum, technology, teaching, and school operations. Because of this, I wouldn't call them "typical" parents; they have extensive knowledge about what happens in our classrooms. Both are questioning whether they should put their precious babies into kindergarten and whether there are better options.

They know that, according to the World Economic Forum (WEF) — a well-respected, international not-for-profit organization that engages leaders from all aspects of society to innovate, collaborate, and find solutions to our greatest problems — there are five skills kids will need in

---

[20] Please see www.parentsengagedineducation.ca

the future:

1. Creativity (problem-solving across disciplines).
2. Digital skills (algorithm design and data handling).
3. Collaboration (self-regulation, understanding others' needs, and working together on complex tasks).
4. Universal citizenship (respect for people of all cultures and embracing diversity, equality, and inclusion).
5. Environmental stewardship (understanding the fragility and finiteness of natural systems and how to interact with them in sustainable ways).

These skills were identified by WEF's *Catalyzing Education 4.0* document,[21] LEGO, the European Commission, and the National Center for O*NET. Unfortunately, these big brains also tell us that less than half of our young people are on track to acquire these skills.[22] For this reason, M and J might delay kindergarten altogether. They might homeschool. Alternatively, they might take a hybrid approach, like our peer and friend "K", also an education leader in Canada:

She and her husband pulled their ten- and twelve-year-old daughters out of school to embark on a year-long learning journey with The World School,[23] during which time they travelled to various countries, exploring different cultures and lands. They wrote and blogged the entire time. They also amassed a portfolio of photographs, and when they returned home, the family held an open house for others interested in The World School. They screened their pics and even cooked and served food from the

---

[21] World Economic Forum (2022): *Catalysing Education 4.0: Investing in the Future of Learning for a Human-Centric Recovery* (https://www3.weforum.org/docs/WEF_Catalysing_Education_4.0_2022.pdf).

[22] World Economic Forum (LinkedIn – 2023): "Investing in childhood skills could contribute $2.54 trillion to the global economy." (www.linkedin.com)

[23] Please see www.theworld.school

countries they had visited.

Along with homeschooling and experiential learning schools like The World School, some parents can look into options that may better meet the needs of their children than traditional educational settings. See the Glossary for more information on…

- Montessori schools.
- Waldorf schools.
- Charter schools.
- Virtual schools.
- Therapeutic schools.

Let's also explore the options that are really "out there":

Artists challenge norms, right? Sure enough, singer-songwriter Alanis Morrisette has gone as far as "unschooling" her children. This is an entirely child-led approach, allowing her children's curiosity to dictate what they learn about and how they spend their time. She "basically gets inside their eyeballs […] constantly watching their eyes and what they're pulled towards, and then [they] do the deep dive."[24] This unstructured education is unconventional, but it gives kids the agency to explore what excites them and lets those interests and passions guide their learning.

Then again, most of us don't have a rockstar life. As fabulous as these (and other) approaches may be, they are also expensive, and not all parents have the ability or setup to provide such opportunities for their children. So, let's focus on what school can be for schoolers with a "normal" setup (i.e., public schooling) can look like for now.

---

[24] Breen, K. (Today.com — 2020): *How singer Alanis Morissette 'unschools' her children* (www.today.com/parents/t177889).

Twin Schools

Maybe there's something about the notion of twin cities we can play with to help bring the privileged and not-so-privileged together more equitably.

"Twin cities" typically refers to two cities that are geographically close to each other and often share cultural, economic, and social ties. These cities may have a special relationship due to their proximity, and may collaborate on various initiatives or projects. An example of twin cities would be Paris and Rome. They are sister cities that engage in cultural exchanges or economic partnerships to foster collaboration and mutual benefit.

Now think of this, but for "twin schools". In many communities, it's usually well-known where the "good" schools (sometimes private schools) are, and where the less desirable ones (sometimes those in lower socioeconomic areas) are. So, what if we created a formalized program for community service on steroids and the schools were paired, just like twin cities? The students could work together to identify the areas of need and figure out how to help each other. That's right, *each other*. By expanding their thinking beyond material things that one school might need to include more immaterial experiences that might benefit the other, like friendship, service, cultural exchanges, personal fulfillment and empathy, communities can be strengthened when they get to know each other and work together, creating positive impact for all. Notably, the students in the "twin schools" would have to be mindful at the outset, to ensure the initiative is stripped of anger and resentment on one side and pride and a sense of ownership on the other.

My vision for "twin schools" is aspirational, but with the resources and commitment from parents and school systems, I think it's doable.

Competency-Based Learning

I will forever wish and keep working for a world where access and privilege are replaced with equality, inclusion, and opportunity for *all* children, without question, and I know M, J, and K will do the same. Unfortunately, school closures, teacher shortages, and the effects of COVID have caused a lot of stress, affecting millions of students and educators worldwide. In 2020 and 2021, for example, the US was hit with one thousand eight hundred and one school closures, affecting just under one million students and sixty thousand teachers across forty-four states. Approximately 1.5% of schools across America have been impacted.[25] Brick-and-mortar school settings are costly, and the pandemic has taught us that we can do things virtually, when appropriate.

In among all this change, we can also begin to consider different learning environments and ways to present content to our children. Little ones need to be monitored in one place, but as students get older, perhaps we can start initiating them into the real world in pragmatized, safe, structured ways.

An educational approach called competency-based learning (CBL) focuses on students mastering specific skills rather than simply completing coursework or accumulating credit hours. What if we coupled this with apprenticeships or mentorships, where students get hands-on experience in their chosen field and switch out sitting in a classroom eight hours a day for real industry experience? With this approach, our future writer "P" (from Chapter 3) would be matched with a writer that could coach and guide him.

Are you thinking, *That's just co-op*? If so: it is, but jacked up. It's co-op *for all students, if* they choose it. We could create student centers or hubs

---

[25] Parks, S.E., Zviedrite, N., Budzyn, S.E., *et al.* (2021): *COVID-19–Related School Closures and Learning Modality Changes* (http://dx.doi.org/10.15585/mmwr.mm7039e2).

where older students curate their own personalized learning plan that is connected to the real world, with the help of CCCs and those already in the roles they would like to pursue. With this approach to education, we wouldn't need as many buildings, nor the setup we have today in our schools.

For early education, I believe big playgrounds are the way to go, like the spectacular Fuji kindergarten setup in Tachikawa, Japan. This unique and innovative learning environment is a circular, open, nature inspired space is built to emphasize play and exploration. No aspirations here: it exists, and it can be replicated.[26] All we need is a huge cultural and economic shift.

With a will, there's a way.

Not everyone in the corporate world wants to mentor, and it can be tough to find good mentors even when there are many options. Training would have to be given to those who would like the opportunity to help young people. They'd also have to be vetted. Mindsets would have to change, tax dollars would have to be allocated, grants would need to be created, and divergent, innovative thinkers would need to come together to ideate and execute. I, for one, am all in to do this work.

Rome wasn't built in a day, and a new school system won't be either. A total rip and repair might not be feasible, but our systems are crumbling, overburdened, stretched, and struggling. Thoughtful, incremental change that puts students at the heart of every single decision made is the way through.

---

[26] Ha, T. (ideas.ted.com—2015): *Inside the world's best kindergarten* (https://ideas.ted.com/inside-the-worlds-best-kindergarten).

Connection, Contribution, Community

As difficult as things may feel while we address the education system's outstanding issues and begin to work on transforming our current reality, teachers can help kids to develop today, in the regular school system. Perhaps when the behaviours we're about to discuss start being integrated and practiced in deep ways (I'm hoping this book is an invitation to those already thinking along these lines), we will have the will to truly shift in meaningful ways that aren't Band-Aid solutions.

At this moment in time, we can start with three topic areas that are a nice tie-in. Educators can already start designing programs to support growth in these areas (some highflyers already are!), and guess what? They take us back to connection and contribution, and then we wrap up with communion.

1. *Connect: Socio-Emotional Learning (SEL) — Understanding Ourselves and Others*

The notion that children should be prepared to become caring, engaged, responsible citizens finds its roots in ancient Greece. In *The Republic*, Plato proposes a holistic curriculum that calls for character development alongside development in the arts, math, science, and physical education.

Jumping ahead to the 1990s, a group of passionate researchers, educators, practitioners, and child advocates created a not-for-profit organization called the Collaborative for Academic, Social, and Emotional Learning (CASEL, or SEL for short) to support the social, emotional, and academic development of all children.[27] It continues to be a world leader

---

[27] Please see https://casel.org/fundamentals-of-sel/

today, providing programming, research, and strategies for the implementation of SEL principles in education systems. SEL has since become a critical element of education.

We know from CASEL research that when students learn to apply the knowledge, skills, and attitudes that we need to understand, manage, and regulate our emotions, they make better decisions and achieve their goals. Furthermore, when they can show empathy for others, they make and maintain good relationships that keep them connected and healthy. SEL positively affects how well kids do in school, their workplace interactions when they leave school, and their coping mechanisms as they manage their stress, mental health, and resilience. Some schools and teachers are seeing this, and are therefore implementing key components of SEL into their curriculum and pedagogy. As per the CASEL framework, these are:

- Self-awareness (to understand our emotions and strengths and where we need to grow).
- Self-management (to regulate emotions, set good goals, and make good choices).
- Social awareness (to understand diversity and others' perspectives).
- Relationship skills, communication, and conflict management.
- Responsible decision-making (for ethical living).

These skills can be taught to our kids so that they have guideposts for *how* to be, in turn creating a much less stressed out and more respectful world. It's up to us to model and help our children practice these components of SEL, so they can become seamless, everyday behaviours.

For now, we can start here: with simple awareness.

2. *Contribute: The Social Development Goals (SDGs) — Taking Care of Each Other and the Planet*

As part of the 2030 Agenda for Sustainable Development, every member of the United Nations adopted a set of seventeen global goals as a universal call to action. These were aimed at ending poverty, protecting planet earth, and creating peace and prosperity for all.[28] These seventeen global goals were:

1. No poverty.
2. No hunger.
3. Good health and wellbeing.
4. Quality education.
5. Gender equality.
6. Clean water and sanitation.
7. Affordable and clean energy.
8. Decent work and economic growth.
9. Industry, innovation, and infrastructure.
10. Reduced inequality.
11. Sustainable cities and communities.
12. Responsible consumption and production.
13. Climate action.
14. Life below water.
15. Life on land.
16. Peace, justice, and strong institutions.
17. Partnerships for the goals.

These goals represent the work we need to do to *undo* what we've done to

---

[28] Please see https://casel.org/fundamentals-of-sel/

the earth and to each other. We're working on gaining greater socioemotional intelligence, as per (1) in this list, but the next step is to apply this to what we're teaching children, so we can build a better future. Forward-thinking, innovative educators are looking for ways to align the curriculum with the SDGs, weaving these important topics into teaching and learning.

Ian Fogarty, a gifted and passionate twelfth grade chemistry and physics teacher in New Brunswick, Canada, is a perfect example of such a forward-thinking and innovative educator. He founded Current Generation to showcase transdisciplinary STEAM-based (science, technology, engineering, art, mathematics) education, and shares his approaches with other educators.[29] His programs are all aligned with national curriculum and the SDGs.

For example, he created a program that teaches students how to make lights and generate a current. This program addresses light poverty, in line with SDG #7 (Clean Energy: Access to Clean Light). It came to be because of a beautiful story about one of his students who, while visiting the Dominican Republic, learned that two young girls she met ("Hailey" and "Maria") couldn't study at night after the day's chores were completed, because, other than candles that burned their hair or kerosene that made them sick, they had no light source. Accordingly, Mr. Fogarty decided to teach his students how to design, solder, build, and 3D print solar lanterns. They shipped five in the first year to the DR. Eight years later (as I write), they have shipped lanterns all over the world. Mr. Fogarty and I have also produced a short film called *Sending Light*, about this program and journey as an exemplar for other educators. The film was written, directed, edited, and shot by film students in York University, Ontario. The story is centered on how the project changed the trajectory of the group of young people who made the lanterns in Mr. Fogarty's physics class and

---

[29] Please see www.currentgeneration.org

showcases how students can change the world when they are connected and committed.

Other online resources and content showing how teachers can integrate the SDGs into their pedagogy are available right now,[30] and the wheels are beginning to turn. Innovative educators have begun this work collaboratively. An example is the #TeachSDGs organization, which connects and supports a community of educators all over the world that have pledged to teach the SDGs.[31]

What's more important than saving the world?

3. *Commune: First Nations, Métis, and Inuit (FMNI) People—Ways of Knowing and Practicing Communion of All Spirits*

Sadly, the mistreatment, displacement, and disrespect of FMNI people is nothing short of tragic. Much healing on both sides of the relationship (us and them) needs to happen so that everyone can embark on a new, deeply meaningful, authentic relationship bound by empathy and respect. In Canada, the Truth and Reconciliation Commission, established in 2008, released a report in 2015 outlining ninety-four calls to action, addressing how we can bring harmony and healing to education, health, justice, language, and culture for FMNI people.[32]

The history of the treatment of these people, particularly in the residential school system we created in Canada in the late nineteenth and twentieth centuries, has had catastrophic effects. The intergenerational

---

[30] Please see https://en.unesco.org/themes/education/sdgs/material
[31] Please see www.teachsdgs.org
[32] Truth and Reconciliation Commission of Canada (2015): *Calls to Action* (https://publications.gc.ca).

trauma resulting from the forced removal of FMNI children through the residential school system, referred to as the "sixties scoop" by Métis social worker Patrick Johnson, combined with centuries of oppressive legislation, has had longstanding and often devasting effects, all in the name of assimilating FMNI people into Euro-Canadian culture.

What was done was incredibly wrong. It's no wonder that many FMNI parents/caregivers still feel distrust and fear toward our school systems.

Canadian colonial education systems are beginning to "do the work", in an attempt to repair the harm we have caused and integrate the Truth and Reconciliation Commission's education related calls to action into their schools. They are providing funding, implementing FMNI curricula, and carrying out teacher training, to address the colonialism in our schools. This is an important process that needs to happen, but we can take it further.

FMNI perspectives and knowledge can help us to unlock an innate cross-cultural understanding about our interconnectedness, with a respect for nature, ceremony, holistic healing, and reciprocity of gifts for the earth, and an emphasis on our relationships, including those with our families, ancestors, and the greater community. We need to remember how to commune with all forms of life so that we can ensure the wellbeing of future generations and the health of our planet. To allow this new understanding to be unlocked, it needs to seep into our curriculum. We need a universal ethical guideline that transcends cultural and religious differences and emphasizes the importance of treating others with dignity, fairness, and empathy in all aspects of life, for the wellbeing of society.

I am not a member of the FMNI community, but I am listening, reflecting, and learning.

Professor Robin Wall Kimmerer, a citizen of the Potawatomi Nation in the US, authored an inspirational book called *Braiding Sweetgrass for Young Adults: Indigenous Wisdom, Scientific Knowledge, and the Teachings of Plants* in 2013. She draws on her indigenous heritage in her writing and research to focus on the relationship between humans and the natural world.

This book was adapted for young adults in 2022 by Monique Gray Smith, a Canadian Cree woman known for her work in FMNI literature in education, and was illustrated by Nicole Niedhart, an FMNI artist.[33] This adaptation is so special. It leads with questions and beautiful artwork to prompt youth in their thinking within the context of FMNI knowledge. It's also a brilliant resource for teachers to use as they revisit their pedagogy with an FMNI perspective.

An example of how we can integrate FMNI perspectives into our teaching pedagogy is Kimmerer's Haudenosaunee Thanksgiving Address. This is a sacred recitation of profound gratitude for the People, Earth Mother, the Waters, the Fish, the Plants, the Food Plants, the Medicine Herbs, the Animals, the Trees, and the Sun. (Notice how they are all capitalized? That's because FMNI people regard them as living and sentient, not as objects.) Here, we give thanks for and acknowledge each of these gifts in the recitation, ending each section with, "Now our minds are one."[34] What a way for children to start each day as Kimmerer suggests, with gratitude, reverence, and respect, in communion with each other and the natural world!

Perhaps our healing journey with the FMNI people can also be the beginning of a healing journey for all of us.

Conclusion: Parents as Partners in Education

For this chapter, I'd like to leave you not with Teacher Talk Tips or questions, but with a call to action.

---

[33] Kimmerer, R. W. (2022): *Braiding Sweetgrass for Young Adults*. Zest Books.
[34] Kimmerer, R. W. (2022): *Braiding Sweetgrass for Young Adults*. Zest Books (p.p. 85–86).

Our ways of being are shifting, and this translates into what we teach our children. The notion of "school" is transforming. Parents have choices and, most importantly, the power to help shape what's to come.

How will you use your voice?

There is no right answer to this question. We can create something together, just like in my favourite folk story, *Stone Soup*:

A hungry traveller comes upon a village and draws the inhabitants out of their homes, who claim that they have little to share. They become curious when he pulls out a cauldron, fills it with water, and heats it over a fire in the center of the village. When they ask what he's doing, he announces he's making stone soup, but it could be so much better with maybe a carrot, onions, and a potato. Soon, each of the villagers contributes one small thing, and eventually, they all enjoy a hearty broth.

This is the power of collaboration, community, contribution, and collective action.

Do you have something you'd like to share, to help reimagine education?

I close with an invitation to join this dialogue. Share your stories, suggestions, and ideas on Instagram at @htttt_cauldron or Facebook page "How to Talk to Teachers", and let's see what we can come up with as one. Be thoughtful and kind, be respectful, and be mindful. Add to the cauldron.

I'll see you there.

ACKNOWLEDGEMENTS

Ask, and the teacher appears. Thank you:

- Karen Grose.
- Camille Rutherford.
- Richard Franz
- David Clarkson.
- Shann McGrail.
- Patricia Gartland.
- Joanne McEachen.

In memory of Mary Stockdale Vernon.

Leap, and the net appears. Thank you:

- Mathilde Torres Gentile.
- Beverly Yates.

In gratitude for those that bring me joy and hold me dear. Thank you:

- Karim Remu.
- Laila Maria Remu.
- Edwin Pericles Remu (woof!).

For helping me along the journey, thank you for your support:

- James E. Kidd.
- Stephanie Southmayd.
- Sabrina Nardone.

- Elysia Circelli.
- Jessica Rizk.
- Robert Iannelli.
- Karen Truyens.
- Martha Jez.
- Nancy Teodoro.
- Tammy Webster.
- Giancarlo Brotto.
- Luigi Ferrara.
- Kaylyn Dorland.
- Ian Fogarty.
- Vince Ranieri.

For my cheerleaders, thank you:
- Natalie Petrella.
- Teresa Tiano.
- Lucy Coschignano.
- Angela Plover.

APPENDIX A
CHATGPT-GENERATED ESSAYS

"Write Me an Essay on the History of Tomato Sauce"

The Culinary Odyssey: A Journey Through the History of Tomato Sauce

Tomato sauce, a staple in kitchens around the world, has a rich and flavorful history that mirrors the global evolution of culinary practices. This ubiquitous condiment, with its versatility and ability to elevate myriad dishes, has roots deeply embedded in the cross-cultural exchange of ingredients and techniques. This essay delves into the fascinating journey of tomato sauce, tracing its origins, development, and impact on global cuisine.

The story of tomato sauce begins in the New World, where indigenous peoples in present-day Mexico cultivated and consumed tomatoes as early as 500 BC. Spanish explorers, including Hernán Cortés, encountered tomatoes during their expeditions in the sixteenth century and brought them back to Europe. After initially being met with skepticism due to its resemblance to poisonous nightshade plants, the tomato slowly gained acceptance as a culinary ingredient.

In Europe, particularly in Italy, the tomato underwent a transformation from a mere curiosity to a culinary star. Initially cultivated as an ornamental plant, Italians gradually integrated tomatoes into their cuisine, giving rise to the iconic tomato sauce. By the eighteenth century, tomato-based recipes appeared in Italian cookbooks, solidifying the tomato's place in Mediterranean culinary traditions.

As tomato sauce gained popularity in Italy, it found its way into French and Mediterranean culinary landscapes. The French incorporated tomatoes into classic sauces like espagnole and marinara, adding depth and richness. Concurrently, Mediterranean cuisines embraced tomato sauce, adapting it to local flavors and preferences and contributing to the diversification of regional culinary identities.

The introduction of tomato sauce to the United States occurred in the early nineteenth century, with its popularity soaring in the immigrant-rich enclaves of cities like New York and Boston. Italian immigrants in particular brought their traditional tomato-based recipes to their new American homes, further integrating tomato sauce into the American culinary repertoire. By the mid-twentieth century, tomato sauce had become a household staple, with iconic American dishes like spaghetti and meatballs becoming widespread.

The twentieth century witnessed the industrialization of tomato sauce production, with companies like Campbell's and Heinz introducing canned varieties. This made tomato sauce more accessible to the masses. The globalization of cuisine further disseminated tomato sauce worldwide, adapting to local tastes and inspiring fusion dishes that transcend cultural boundaries.

Today, tomato sauce continues to be a culinary linchpin, featuring prominently in diverse cuisines, from Italian and Mexican to Indian and Chinese. The rise of gourmet and artisanal products has elevated the quality and variety of tomato sauces available, providing consumers with options ranging from traditional recipes to innovative flavor combinations.

The history of tomato sauce is a testament to the interconnectedness of cultures and the transformative power of culinary evolution. From its humble beginnings in the New World to its integration into global cuisines, tomato sauce has become an indispensable component of countless dishes, transcending borders and enriching the world's culinary tapestry. As we savor the tangy sweetness of tomato sauce in our meals, we partake in a culinary legacy shaped by centuries of innovation, adaptation, and shared flavors.

"Write Me an Essay on the Origin of Tomato Sauce, in Shakespearean Language"

In the annals of culinary history, the genesis of tomato sauce doth unfold like a theatrical spectacle upon the grand stage of gastronomy. Verily, 'tis a tale that hath its roots entwined with the New World, where the plump and scarlet fruit of the tomato didst make its entrance into the kitchens of Europe during the late sixteenth century.

In the days of yore, ere the tomato didst grace the shores of the Old World, European palates had ne'er encountered this luscious nightshade. Native to the realm of the Aztecs, it was during the explorative voyages of Christopher Columbus that the tomato found its way into the hands of Europeans. Aye, Columbus did bring back this curious fruit from the bountiful lands of the Americas, yet 'twas met with skepticism, for many deemed it poisonous and shunned its consumption.

As time unfurled its wings, the tomato gained acceptance and gradually found its place within the culinary repertoire of the Old World. The Italian peninsula, with its rich culinary heritage, played a pivotal role in transforming the tomato from an exotic oddity to a celebrated ingredient. The inception of tomato sauce, that ambrosial elixir which doth grace countless dishes with its sumptuous presence, can be traced to Italy's embrace of the tomato.

125

The grand dame of Italian cuisine, Catherine de' Medici, is oft attributed with introducing the tomato to the courts of France. Her marriage to Henry II in 1533 didst bring about an amalgamation of Italian and French culinary traditions, and the tomato, with its bold hues and robust flavors, became a star in the gastronomic firmament.

Tomato sauce, in its earliest incarnations, was a simple concoction, a marriage of tomatoes, garlic, and olive oil. 'Twas in the crucible of Italian kitchens that this alchemy took place, as culinary artisans experimented with herbs and spices to craft a symphony of flavors. The tomato sauce, once a humble accompaniment, transformed into a culinary masterpiece that graced the tables of nobility and commoners alike.

As the centuries unfolded, tomato sauce spread its wings beyond the borders of Italy, permeating the culinary landscapes of Europe and beyond. The New World, from whence the tomato hailed, embraced this sauce with open arms, integrating it into the culinary mosaic of diverse cuisines.

In conclusion, the origin of tomato sauce is a tale replete with the adventurous spirit of exploration and the alchemy of culinary creativity. From the verdant fields of the Americas to the bustling kitchens of Europe, the tomato sauce hath traversed time and space to become an indispensable companion to myriad dishes. Let us, therefore, raise a toast to the tomato and its saucy transformation, a saga that hath enriched the tapestry of culinary history with its vibrant hues and delectable flavors.

APPENDIX B
PARENTAL CONTROL AND
SCREEN TIME APPLICATIONS

There are several apps that offer features to help users monitor and manage their screen time. Many also offer parental control options. Here are a few examples:

1. Screen time. Introduced by Apple in iOS 12, this is designed to help users better understand and manage their device usage, particularly for parents managing their children's screen time. Features include detailed activity reports on how much time users spend on devices, app limits, downtime, content and privacy restrictions, and passcodes.

2. Google Family Link. Developed by Google, Family Link allows parents to set screen time limits, view activity reports, remotely lock devices, and manage app installations for their children's Android devices.

3. Microsoft family. A set of features and services provided by Microsoft to help families manage and monitor their digital lives across various devices and platforms.

4. OurPact. Offers parental control features for both iOS and Android devices. Parents can set screen time limits, block specific apps or websites, schedule device usage, and track device location.

5. Qustodio. A comprehensive parental control app available for iOS, Android, Windows, Mac, and Kindle devices. It offers features such as screen time limits, app blocking, website filtering, and location tracking.

6. Net Nanny. A parental control solution available across multiple

platforms. It provides features like app blocking, web filtering, screen time management, and remote monitoring of online activity.

7. Bark. A monitoring app that helps parents keep track of their children's online activities across various platforms and devices. It uses advanced algorithms to detect potential issues like cyberbullying, online predators, and explicit content.

APPENDIX C
THE GLOBAL LEARNING COMPETENCIES

The concept of global competencies has evolved through the collaborative efforts of individuals, organizations, and educational thinkers who recognize the necessity of preparing individuals to navigate and contribute meaningfully to a globally interconnected world. The development of global competencies is an ongoing process, reflecting the dynamic nature of the challenges and opportunities presented by globalization.

Various organizations, scholars, and educational thinkers have contributed to the development and promotion of the idea of global competencies.[35] International organizations such as UNESCO (United Nations Educational, Scientific and Cultural Organization) and the OECD (Organisation for Economic Co-operation and Development) have played significant roles in advancing global competencies in education. UNESCO, for example, has emphasized global citizenship education and the development of competencies that enable individuals to understand and engage with global issues.

Scholars and researchers in the fields of education, international relations, and global studies have also contributed to the conceptualization of global competencies. Various frameworks, including twenty-first century skills frameworks, highlight the importance of skills such as critical thinking, communication, collaboration, and cultural

---

[35] *Global Competencies: Pan-Canadian Systems-Level Framework on Global Competencies* (www.globalcompetencies.cmec.ca/ global-competencies).

competence.

Currently, the global competencies are:

1. Critical thinking and problem-solving. This is the ability to analyze complex issues, think critically, and solve problems creatively. Students should be able to apply these skills to real-world challenges and address complex issues and problems by acquiring, processing, analyzing, and interpreting information to make informed judgments and decisions. Critical thinking and problem-solving means engaging in cognitive processes to understand and resolve problems and having the willingness to achieve one's potential as a constructive and reflective citizen. Learning is deepened when it is situated in meaningful, real-world, authentic experiences.

2. Innovation, creativity, and entrepreneurship. This involves the ability to turn ideas into action, meet the needs of a community, and enhance concepts, ideas, or products, all with the purpose of contributing new solutions for complex economic, social, and environmental problems. It involves leadership, taking risks, independent/unconventional thinking, and experimenting with new strategies, techniques, or perspectives through inquiry research and building and scaling ideas sustainably.

3. Interpersonal skills, self-reflection, and self-direction. Students should develop self-awareness and an understanding of their own values, biases, and cultural identity. Reflective practices contribute to personal growth and a deeper understanding of one's role in a global context. Students should become aware of and demonstrate agency in their process of learning, and should develop dispositions that support motivation, perseverance, resilience, and self-regulation. Students should believe in their ability to learn (growth mindset) and develop strategies for planning, monitoring, and reflecting on one's past, present, and future goals, potential actions and strategies, and results.

Self-reflection and thinking about thinking (metacognition) promote lifelong learning, adaptive capacity, wellbeing, and the transfer of learning in an ever-changing world.

4. Collaboration, teamwork, and leadership. This involves the interplay of the cognitive (including thinking and reasoning), interpersonal, and intrapersonal competencies necessary to participate effectively and ethically in teams. Ever-increasing versatility and depth of skill is applied across diverse situations, roles, groups, and perspectives, to co-construct knowledge, meaning, and content, and learn from and with others in physical and virtual environments.

5. Communication and language skills. Proficiency in multiple languages and effective communication skills are crucial for navigating global contexts. This includes not only linguistic abilities, but also the capacity to communicate ideas clearly and respectfully across cultural and linguistic boundaries. It involves receiving and expressing meaning (e.g., reading and writing, viewing and creating, and listening and speaking) in different contexts, to different audiences, for different purposes. Effective communication involves understanding both local and global perspectives, societal and cultural contexts, and using a variety of media appropriately, responsibly, and safely, with regard to one's digital footprint.

6. Global citizenship and sustainability. Global citizens understand their responsibility to contribute positively to the world. This includes ethical decision-making, social responsibility, and an awareness of the global impact of individual and collective action. It involves reflecting on diverse worldviews and perspectives and understanding and addressing ecological, social, and economic issues that are crucial to living in a contemporary, connected, interdependent, and sustainable world. It also includes the acquisition of the knowledge, motivations, dispositions, and skills required for an ethos of engaged citizenship,

with an appreciation for the diversity of people and their perspectives. It entails the ability to envision and work toward a better and more sustainable future for all.

7. Cultural awareness and sensitivity. Understanding and respecting diverse cultures, beliefs, and perspectives is fundamental to global competence. Students should develop an awareness of their own cultural biases and appreciation for the richness of cultural diversity.

8. Global citizenship and ethical responsibility. Global citizens understand their responsibility to contribute positively to the world. This includes ethical decision-making, social responsibility, and an awareness of the global impact of individual and collective action.

9. Global economic and political awareness. Solid understanding of global economic systems, geopolitical events, and international relations is crucial for informed global citizenship. This includes awareness of social justice issues and economic disparities.

10. Technology literacy. Proficiency in using technology for communication, research, and collaboration is a crucial global competency. This involves not only technical skills, but also a critical understanding of the ethical and social implications of technology.

11. Flexibility and adaptability. The ability to adapt to different cultural contexts and navigate change is vital. Global competencies include being flexible, open minded, and resilient in the face of diverse challenges.

12. Environmental sustainability. A global perspective encompasses an understanding of environmental issues and the importance of sustainable practices. Students should be aware of the impact of human activities on the planet and explore solutions for a sustainable future.

13. Empathy and intercultural competence. Global competencies involve developing empathy and intercultural competence. This includes the ability to connect with people from different backgrounds, recognize

and appreciate diverse perspectives, and navigate intercultural interactions with respect and understanding.

APPENDIX D

BOOK EVALUATION RUBRIC

Disclaimer: Some components have been generated by ChatGPT.

Book Title: *How to Talk to Teachers*

Evaluator:

Date:

Criteria	Excellent (4)	Good (3)	Fair (2)	Needs Improvement (1)
Content	Comprehensive and rich in detail. The content is highly relevant, engaging, and thought provoking.	Solid content with clear relevance. The book covers the main points effectively.	Adequate content, but some areas lack depth or clarity.	Content is weak or irrelevant and does not effectively convey the intended message.
Writing Style	Engaging and compelling. The writing style is captivating, enhancing the overall reading experience.	Well written, with good flow and clarity. The writing style enhances the reader's experience.	Adequate writing style, but some areas lack clarity or are not engaging.	Writing style is weak, making it difficult for the reader to follow or stay engaged.
Organization	Logical and well structured. The book has a clear and effective organization that enhances understanding.	Well organized, with a logical flow of ideas. Transitions are smooth and support comprehension.	Adequate organization, but some sections lack coherence. Transitions are somewhat abrupt.	Poor organization, making it challenging to follow the structure of the book.

Character Development (If Applicable)	Characters are well developed, with depth, complexity, and growth throughout the narrative.	Characters are developed, with some depth and growth evident.	Characters are somewhat underdeveloped, and their growth is limited.	Characters lack depth and show little or no growth.
Themes and Messages	Themes are well-explored and contribute significantly to the overall impact of the book.	Themes are evident and contribute to the overall impact of the book.	Themes are present but not fully developed or explored.	Themes are unclear or poorly developed, detracting from the overall impact.
Language and Vocabulary	Rich and varied language. Vocabulary enhances the overall quality of the writing.	Clear and appropriate language with a good choice of vocabulary.	Language is basic or repetitive, with limited use of varied vocabulary.	Language is unclear, inappropriate, or excessively repetitive.
Pacing	Pacing is well managed, contributing to a balanced and engaging reading experience.	Pacing is generally good, with minor inconsistencies.	Pacing is inconsistent, affecting the overall reading experience.	Pacing is erratic, making it difficult for readers to stay engaged.
Visual Elements (If Applicable)	Visual elements (e.g., illustrations and graphs) enhance and complement the text effectively.	Visual elements are present and support the content adequately.	Visual elements are present but do not significantly enhance the content.	Lack of visual elements, or visuals do not contribute positively to the book.
Overall Impact	The book leaves a lasting impression, provoking thought and evoking strong emotions.	The book has a positive impact and resonates with the reader.	The impact is moderate, with some memorable aspects.	The overall impact is weak and the book fails to leave a lasting impression.

APPENDIX E
SUPPORTED EDUCATION
AND DIFFABILITIES

Supported education refers to educational programs and support services designed to meet the unique needs of students with diffabilities and supported needs. These needs can encompass a wide range of challenges, including learning diffabilities, intellectual diffabilities, physical diffabilities, developmental delays, behavioural disorders, sensory impairments, and other health impairments. The goal of supported education is to provide students with the necessary accommodations, modifications, and individualized instruction to help them succeed academically, socially, and emotionally.

Key aspects of supported education include:

- Individualized education plans (IEPs). Students with diffabilities are typically provided with an IEP, which is a personalized plan outlining their specific learning goals, instructional strategies, support services, and accommodations. The IEP is developed collaboratively by educators, parents or guardians, and other relevant professionals, and it is regularly reviewed and updated to ensure the student's needs are being met.

- Differentiated instruction. Supported education teachers and support staff employ various instructional strategies and techniques to meet the diverse needs of students with diffabilities. These may include adapting the curriculum, using multisensory approaches, providing visual aids, offering additional support or reinforcement, and utilizing assistive technologies.

- Related services. In addition to academic instruction, students with diffabilities receive related services to address their individual needs. These services can include speech therapy, occupational therapy, physical therapy, counseling, social skills training, and behaviour intervention.
- Inclusive practices. Supported education aims to promote the inclusion and participation of students with diffabilities in the general education environment, to the maximum extent possible. Inclusive practices involve providing appropriate supports and accommodations (to ensure that students with diffabilities have equal access to educational opportunities and are integrated into classroom activities and social interactions with their peers).
- Collaboration and support. Supported education often involves collaboration among educators, specialists, parents or guardians, and other stakeholders to ensure that students receive comprehensive support and services. This collaboration may include regular communication, team meetings, professional development, and coordination of resources.
- Transition planning. For students with diffabilities who are transitioning to adulthood, supported education may include transition planning to help them prepare for postsecondary education, vocational training, employment, and independent living. Transition planning focuses on developing skills, exploring career options, and accessing community resources to support successful transitions.

APPENDIX F
AI-GENERATED LESSON PLAN: EXPLORING TIGERS

"Create a Lesson Plan on Tigers for Kindergarten"

Grade level: Kindergarten

Subject: Science and social studies

Objective: Students will learn about tigers, including their appearance, habitat, diet, and behaviour. Students will develop an appreciation for the importance of protecting tigers and their habitats.

Materials: Pictures or books about tigers; videos or online resources about tigers; construction paper; crayons or markers; glue; scissors; tiger plush toys or figurines (optional).

Lesson duration: Approximately forty-five minutes

1. Introduction (10 Minutes)

Begin the lesson by gathering students in a circle or at a designated meeting area.

Show pictures or videos of tigers and ask the students if they know what animal it is.

Engage the students in a brief discussion about tigers. Ask questions such as:

- What do you know about tigers?
- Where do tigers live?
- What do tigers eat?
- What colour are tigers?

Explain to the students that they will be learning more about tigers during the lesson.

2. Learn About Tigers (15 Minutes)

Read a children's book about tigers or show a short video about tigers in their natural habitat.

Discuss key facts about tigers, including their appearance, habitat, diet, and behaviour. Use simple language and visuals to help the students understand.

3. Tiger Craft Activity (15 Minutes)

Distribute construction paper, crayons or markers, glue, and scissors to each student.

Instruct the students to create their own tiger masks or tiger drawings. They can use the provided materials to cut out tiger shapes from the construction paper, decorate them with stripes and facial features, and glue on any additional details.

Encourage the students to be creative and use their imaginations while making their tiger crafts.

4. *Wrap Up and Discussion (5 Minutes)*

Gather the students back together to discuss what they learned about tigers.

Ask the students to share their tiger crafts with the class and explain why they chose to create them the way they did.

Reinforce key concepts about tigers and their importance in the wild.

Emphasize the importance of protecting tigers and their habitats to ensure their survival for future generations.

5. *Extension Activity (Optional)*

If time allows, invite the students to explore tiger themed books or educational games during free play time.

Encourage the students to continue learning about tigers at home by reading books or watching videos about these majestic animals with their families.

Assessment

Informal assessment can be conducted through observation during discussions, craft activities, and student participation.

Assess students' understanding of key concepts about tigers based on their responses during the lesson and their ability to create accurate tiger crafts.

Note to Teacher

Be sure to provide a supportive and inclusive learning environment, adapting activities as needed to accommodate individual student needs and abilities.

Use age-appropriate language and visuals to engage the students and make the lesson accessible to all learners.

Encourage curiosity and exploration throughout the lesson to foster a love for learning about animals and the natural world.

GLOSSARY

Disclaimer: Some definitions have been generated by ChatGPT.

Chapter 2

Accessibility

The design and provision of products, services, and environments that are usable and accessible to individuals with disabilities or diverse needs. Aims to ensure equal access and participation for all people, regardless of their abilities or limitations.

AI Hallucinations

An expression used to describe instances where artificial intelligence systems produce unexpected or erroneous outputs, often resembling hallucinations or distortions of reality. May occur due to flaws in the AI model or data, leading to unintended results.

Algorithm

A set of instructions or rules followed by a computer program to perform a specific task or solve a problem. Can be simple or complex. Fundamental to computer science and programming.

ChatGPT

An advanced conversational AI model developed by OpenAI, capable of generating human-like text based on the input it receives. Part of the GPT (Generative Pre-Trained Transformer) series of language models.

Critical Thinking

The process of actively and skillfully conceptualizing, analyzing, and evaluating information to form well reasoned judgements and make informed decisions. Involves questioning assumptions, considering alternative perspectives, and applying logic and evidence to solve problems.

Cybersecurity

The practice of protecting computer systems, networks, and data from unauthorized access, attacks, and breaches. Encompasses strategies, technologies, and policies aimed at safeguarding digital assets and ensuring the confidentiality, integrity, and availability of information.

Cyberspace

The virtual environment or digital realm created by interconnected computer networks. Encompasses the Internet, online platforms, and digital communication channels where information is exchanged and accessed.

Data Analytics

The process of examining large datasets to uncover patterns, trends, and insights that can inform decision-making and improve outcomes. Involves collecting, processing, analyzing, and interpreting data using statistical and computational techniques.

Digital Literacy

The ability to effectively navigate, evaluate, and communicate information in digital contexts. Includes skills such as using technological tools, critically evaluating online content, and responsibly engaging in digital communication and collaboration.

Facebook LLaMa

Facebook Large Language Model Meta. A significant language model developed by Meta (previously known as Facebook) to support researchers in advancing their endeavors within the field of artificial intelligence. Functions as a conversational tool, enabling users to engage in dialogue and receive AI-generated responses to inquiries.

Gaming in Education

The integration of gaming principles, mechanics, and technologies into educational settings to enhance teaching and learning outcomes. Leverages the immersive and interactive nature of games to promote skill development, motivation, and engagement among students.

Google Gemini

An artificial intelligence model that can understand and generate text, images, video, audio, and code. A multimodal model that can complete complex tasks in various domains. Developed by Google's AI research labs DeepMind and Google Research.

HAL-9000

A fictional artificial intelligence character in Arthur C. Clarke's *Space Odyssey* series and Stanley Kubrick's film adaptation, known for its advanced cognitive abilities and ominous behaviour.

Personalized Learning

An educational approach that tailors instruction, content, and pace to the individual needs, interests, and abilities of each learner. Utilizes technology and data to provide customized learning experiences and maximize student engagement and achievement.

Turnitin

A widely used plagiarism detection and academic integrity tool used in educational institutions to check student submissions for originality and proper citation. Compares submitted documents against a vast database of academic and online sources to identify potential instances of plagiarism.

Chapter 3

Abraham Maslow

An American psychologist best known for his theory of human motivation, often represented as Maslow's hierarchy of needs. Born on April 1, 1908, in Brooklyn, New York, Maslow made significant contributions to the fields of psychology and education.

Maslow's hierarchy of needs is a psychological theory that suggests human needs can be arranged in a hierarchical order, with basic, fundamental needs at the bottom and higher-level, more complex needs at the top. The hierarchy is typically represented as a pyramid with five levels:

1. Physiological needs. At the base of the hierarchy are the physiological needs necessary for human survival, including air, water, food, shelter, sleep, and reproduction.
2. Safety needs. Once physiological needs are satisfied, individuals seek

safety and security. This encompasses personal and financial security, health, and protection from accidents or harm.

3. Love and belongingness needs. The third level involves social needs, such as the desire for love, affection, belongingness, and meaningful relationships with others.

4. Esteem needs. Esteem needs focus on gaining a sense of self-worth, confidence, and recognition, and the desire for achievement and respect from others.

5. Self-actualization. At the top of the pyramid is the concept of self-actualization, representing the fulfillment of personal potential, self-discovery, creativity, and the realization of one's capabilities.

Maslow's theory suggests that individuals are motivated to fulfill these needs in a sequential manner, starting from the bottom of the hierarchy and moving upward. Notably, Maslow proposed that individuals must satisfy lower-level needs before higher-level needs become prominent motivators.

Joanne Mceachen

As of January 2022, Joanne McEachen is associated with the concept of contributive learning. Contributive learning is a framework focused on transforming education by placing learners at the center of the process. This approach emphasizes the idea that every student has the capacity to contribute meaningfully to their own education and the learning community as a whole.

Key principles of contributive learning include:

- Empowerment (i.e., empowering students to take an active role in their learning journey). This involves fostering a sense of agency, self-efficacy, and ownership over their educational experiences.

- Collaboration (i.e., promoting collaborative learning environments where students work together, share ideas, and contribute to each other's learning). Collaboration is seen as a key element in the development of twenty-first century skills.

- Real-world connections (i.e., integrating learning experiences that connect to real-world contexts and issues). Contributive learning aims to make education relevant to students' lives and the broader global context.

- Inclusion (i.e., ensuring that all students, regardless of background or ability, have the opportunity to contribute and participate meaningfully in the learning process). This aligns with the principles of inclusivity and diversity.

- Continuous growth (i.e., supporting continuous growth and development for both students and educators). Contributive learning encourages a growth mindset and a commitment to lifelong learning.

- Global perspective (i.e., emphasizing a global perspective and encouraging students to consider their role as contributors, not only to their local communities, but also to the broader global community).

Joanne McEachen, through her work with The Learner First, has advocated for the implementation of contributive learning principles in educational systems. The Learner First is an organization that focuses on transforming education by prioritizing the needs and experiences of learners.

It's important to note that educational frameworks and initiatives may evolve, so for the most current and detailed information about Joanne McEachen's work and contributive learning, it's advisable to refer to more recent sources or to directly explore publications and resources associated with her and The Learner First.

Project-Based Learning

Project-based learning (PBL) is an instructional approach where students engage in hands-on, real-world projects to develop their knowledge and skills through active exploration and inquiry. In project-based learning, students work collaboratively to investigate and respond to complex questions, challenges, or problems, often with a focus on solving authentic, meaningful problems or addressing issues relevant to their lives or communities.

Key features of project-based learning include:

- Real-world relevance. The projects are designed to be authentic and relevant to the students' lives, interests, and communities, allowing them to see the practical applications of their learning.

- Inquiry and exploration. Students engage in inquiry driven learning, where they pose questions, conduct research, and explore multiple perspectives to deepen their understanding of the topic or problem.

- Hands-on activities. The projects involve hands-on, experiential tasks that require students to actively apply their knowledge and skills to solve problems, design solutions, or create products.

- Collaborative learning. Students work collaboratively in teams or groups to plan, implement, and reflect on their projects, fostering communication, teamwork, and interpersonal skills.

- Authentic assessment. Assessment in project-based learning focuses on students' abilities to demonstrate understanding, apply skills, and produce tangible artifacts or solutions, rather than rote memorization or standardized tests.

- Student autonomy and voice. Project-based learning empowers students to take ownership of their learning by allowing them to make decisions, set goals, and pursue areas of interest within the project framework.

- Integration of disciplines. The projects often integrate multiple subject areas, allowing students to make connections and see the interdisciplinary nature of real-world problems and solutions.

Chapter 6

Alternative Schools

Alternative schools are educational institutions that provide nontraditional approaches to learning and often cater to students who may not thrive in traditional mainstream educational settings. These schools offer alternative curricula, teaching methods, and environments to better meet the diverse needs of students who may require different educational approaches for various reasons.

Here are some common types of alternative schools:

- Montessori schools. Based on the educational philosophy of Maria Montessori, these schools emphasize self-directed learning, mixed-age classrooms, and hands-on, experiential learning.
- Waldorf schools. Inspired by Rudolf Steiner's philosophy, Waldorf schools focus on holistic education, integrating academics with artistic and practical activities and emphasizing the development of imagination and creativity.
- Charter schools. These publicly funded schools operate independently of traditional school districts and often have more flexibility in their curriculum, teaching methods, and organizational structure.
- Online schools. Also known as virtual schools or cyber schools, these institutions offer online courses and instruction, providing flexibility and accessibility for students who may have difficulty attending traditional brick-and-mortar schools.

- Therapeutic schools. These schools specialize in providing education and support for students with emotional, behavioural, or developmental challenges, often integrating therapy and counseling services into the educational program.
- Homeschooling. Homeschooling involves parents or guardians educating their children at home, often following a customized curriculum tailored to the child's individual needs and interests.
- Experiential learning schools. These schools focus on hands-on, project-based learning, often incorporating real-world experiences and community engagement into the curriculum.

Alternative schools aim to provide educational opportunities that better meet the needs of diverse learners, offering alternatives to traditional approaches and environments that may not be suitable for all students. They can be valuable options for students who may struggle academically, socially, or emotionally in traditional schools, providing tailored support and opportunities for success.

ABOUT THE AUTHOR

Lia De Cicco Remu is a certified teacher with over fifteen years of experience in national education leadership for Canada in the EdTech industry. She is devoted to connecting and collaborating with people to make this new world a better place for children, so that they all shine brightly.

Lia lives in Toronto, Canada, with her husband, daughter, and puppy, Edwin Pericles.

She loves to hear from her readers. Visit her Instagram at @htttt_cauldron or her Facebook page "How to Talk to Teachers".

Printed in the USA
CPSIA information can be obtained
at www.ICGtesting.com
LVHW041049230824
789024LV00004B/87